"This is what Heaven's going to look like!" – C.K.

"Keep glowing and growing so that others might follow in your steps and help increase open doors for the extended family. What a challenging ministry!" – M.G.

"It's exciting to see how you and Neal followed God's leading. Hearing His voice and obeying are often two very separate acts! Praise God for you and your family." – K.W.

"Your ability to reflect the love you have for your children, your quiet humor, and your peaceful nature all reinforce your message of letting God direct our lives." – K.M.

"You speak to a lot of hearts. Great things are in store for you as you continue to leave yourself available for God's direction." – C.B.

"You are a beautiful witness to motherhood! God bless you and your great family." – P.D.

"You minister to many hearts. Your message gives many women encouragement as well as inspiration." – K.S.

"I have been reliving your wonderful story over and over. It still brings tears to my eyes. Thank you for your love and obedience to the Lord." – C.V.

"What a great love you've expressed and trust in a great God too. Women need to hear this message as a challenge for a deeper faith and closer walk with the Lord." – J.G.

"Many people were thrilled to hear how God has gone before you all the way. Thank you for the model you and your family are to our congregation. You are much loved!" – D.VB., Pastor

"You are a special Mom and you have a special ministry to your family. I admire you and I know God is blessing you and other people through you. Keep up the good work!" D.M.

"Your personal story is an inspiring one in reaching out to help others. Thank you for providing the spark!" – P.W.

"Your wit and wisdom as you share your unique family is a delight. You are right. God does have a sense of humor, and your lively family from around the world is proof indeed. Thanks for giving us a glimpse of your Lord's daily intervention into the lives of His children." – P.P.

"You have a unique and wonderful story and the complete sincerity of your message has an impact on anyone who hears it." – D.B.

"We were all encouraged to share our love a little more fully after hearing how your family has learned to share so much with so many. May God continue to bless you and your ever-growing family as you share His love with others around you!" – D.T.

"We were encouraged by your message of inspiration as well as humor as you shared the ups and downs, successes and errors of parenting your special kids. What an incredible story!" – W.C.

"I know many have and will receive blessings of eternity because of you. You are a <u>special lady</u>!" – H.M.

"We want to hear *more* of your story and testimony! You really are an inspiration to me, especially in how willing you are to accept whatever God brings into your life…and always with a smile!" – K.R.

God's Best to Beverly – you led the way! I hope you enjoy our story.

Eight Was Not Enough

The Unlikely Adventures of an Only Child

by

Jeannie Satre

♡ Jeannie Satre
Ps. 115:1

ACW Press
5501 N. 7th Ave. #502
Phoenix, AZ 85013
Jeannie35@juno.com

Cover design by Eric Walljasper
Page design by Steven R. Laube
Typeset using Electra 12pt. Designed in 1935 by William Addision Dwiggins, Electra has been a standard book typeface since its release because of its evenness of design and high legibility.

Unless otherwise noted, all Scripture quotations are from the *Holy Bible*, New International Version, copyright © 1973, 1978, 1984 by International Bible Society. Used by permission of Zondervan Publishing House. All rights reserved.

Scripture quotations marked NASB are taken from *The New American Standard Bible*, © 1960, 1962, 1963, 1968, 1971, 1972, 1975, 1977 by the Lockman Foundation. Used by permission.

Scripture quotations marked TEV are taken from The Good News Bible, The Bible in Today's English Version © 1966, 1971, 1976 by the American Bible Society. Used by permission.

Scripture quotations marked NLT are taken from the *Holy Bible*, New Living Translation, © 1996. Used by permission of Tyndale House Publishers, Inc., Wheaton, Illinois 60189. All rights reserved.

Publisher's Cataloging-in-Publication
(Provided by Quality Books, Inc.)

Satre, Jeanne M.
    Eight was not enough : the unlikely adventures of an only child / by Jeanne M. Satre — 1st ed.
    p. cm.
    Includes bibliographical references.
    ISBN 0-9656749-5-9

    1. Special needs adoption--Anecdotes. 2. Interracial adoption--Anecdotes. 3. Family--United States.   I. Title

HV875.55.S27 1998   306.87'4'092
                        QBI97-41613

Printed in the United States of America

To obtain more copies please contact:
Jeannie Satre
401 Gregory Lane Suite 112
Pleasant Hill, CA 94523
See the order form in the back of this book.

Dedication

To Neal, my partner in life, love, faith, adventure
and, more recently, Hagen-Das bars.
None of this could have happened without you!

And to each one of my children who have given me
immeasurable joy. I love you. You're the BEST!

About the Author

Jeannie Satre, a native Californian is a resident of Walnut Creek California. Educated at the University of California at Davis and California State University at San Francisco, she taught school in the Bay area.

She and her husband, Neal, are the parents of a large international family (nine!), including several children who are physically challenged. Some of their children came from Mother Teresa in India.

As advocates for children and adoption, the Satres served for fifteen years on the Board of Directors of "A.A.S.K." (Adopt a Special Kid) a national adoption agency. Jeannie, herself, is adopted.

In addition to television interviews, Jeannie and her family have been featured in several newspaper and magazine articles.

Jeannie is a graduate of C.L.A.S.S. (Christian Leadership and Speaker's Seminar), has enjoyed many years in Bible Study Fellowship and Community Bible Study, has completed the Disability Awareness Program through her county's Superintendent of Schools, and served four years on the Board of Directors of the California Women's Retreat.

Currently Jeannie is teaching a large weekly Women's Bible Study at her church. She also speaks for churches and Christian Women's Clubs throughout northern California. For fun Jeannie loves Gospel singing, snorkeling in warm blue water, visiting Bed and breakfasts and every kind of travel!

If your community organization, church or women's ministry is interested in considering the author as a speaker for a women's conference, retreat, or banquet, please contact:

Jeannie Satre
401 Gregory Lane, Suite 112
Pleasant Hill, CA 94523
(925) 939-1991
www.adoptedfamily.com

Heartfelt Thanks to:

Jesus Christ who gave me new life and designed our family...beyond my wildest imagination.

My wonderful husband Neal who believes in me and wouldn't let me "give up" my writing.

Grandma Bertha Holt and Mother Teresa who arranged loving care for many of our children until they could "come home."

My faithful friends who pray for me and my family.

Dorothy Atwood DeBolt who inspired us in adoption and then cheered us on!

Elsie Chapman who guided me through children's surgeries, crutches, braces and made it seem easy.

Colleen Townsend Evans, my example.

Eric Hill who believed in my story.

Lucinda Vardey who helped me start writing.

Elaine Wright Colvin who encouraged and directed me.

And to Steve Laube, my editor and publisher, who put all of my work together.

Each one of you are an invaluable gift! God is good...all the time!!

Circle of Love

Our family is a circle of love and strength.
With every birth and every union the circle grows.
Every joy shared adds more love.
Every crisis faced together makes the circle stronger.

Author Unknown

"For I know the plans I have for you,"
declares the Lord,
"Plans to prosper you and not harm you,
plans to give you hope and a future."

Jeremiah 29:11

1

The familiar smell of the hospital struck a feeling of dread in me. I announced through the intercom, "Rebecca's foster Mother."

Anxiously peering into each cubicle, I spied "my girl," her frail 60 lbs. lost in the sheets. Twenty year old college students were a rarity in Cardiac Intensive Care. Despite Muscular Dystrophy, she had far surpassed her ten year life expectancy.

"Hi Mom." Laboring for breath she attempted her usual cheerfulness. "I'm crummy. Dr. Hunt is talking about the respirator."

Fear overcame me as she remembered her past. "If I'm on it again I might never get off."

With a power wheelchair for mobility, Rebecca lived the hectic student life. Could she endure living on a respirator? "She's yours Jesus! 10% lung capacity has caused her to suffer so much," I mused. Dr. Hunt's arrival jarred me. This compassionate man...our hero.

"There's just no improvement," he drawled. "And after five weeks! The respirator could be our only option now. I'll explain it all to her."

Rebecca would choose. Black coffee soothed me momentarily. "O Lord. You love Rebecca. Guide her choice and please heal her."

"Rebecca's going for it! It's not long term, maybe a week or two."

When my husband Neal and I returned to CICU our hearts ached for Rebecca. Lying flat, the plastic tube that filled her mouth prevented any speech.

Characteristically, she waved, pointing the red "ET" heart light taped to her finger.

"Just rest, Rebecca."

"Neal, she's *so* tiny. Nurses can't appreciate her. They're preoccupied with machines. I'm bringing a sign!" So the next day she was "labeled!"

"Rebecca - UCD Jr., psych major, drama enthusiast, legion of friends, kid of the King." Plus two hearts; we love you and God loves you!

Day after day I drove 3 hours to sit with Rebecca and still heard, "About the same." Many prayers upheld her and the Psalms soothed me as I watched her sleep.

> "For He will command His angels concern-
> ing you to guard you in all your ways;
> they will lift you up in their hands"...
> "Because he loves me," says the Lord,
> "I will rescue him; I will protect him,
> for he acknowledges my name. He will call
> upon me and I will answer him; I will be
> with him in trouble, I will deliver him
> and honor him. With long life will I satisfy
> him and show him my salvation."
> (Psalm 91:11-12, 15-16)

Sustaining words! Her room overflowed with greetings while the love of her college friends surrounded her.

One day while opened to Jeremiah, God gave me words I'll never forget.

"Do not be afraid...for I am with you and will rescue you, declares the Lord."

A promise for Rebecca!

That same day, Dr. Hunt greeted me. "Hopefully, we've turned the corner."

Gradually Rebecca improved. And two weeks later God performed the ultimate miracle. Grasping the receiver, a tiny, raspy voice surprised me, "Hi Mom! I'm off!"

"Oh thank you Jesus."

"It wasn't even hard. I got right off! Boy, Dr. Hunt is happy!"

During our next visit two cheerful IV specialists arrived hoping to find her illusive veins. Noticing Rebecca's "sign" they responded, "Oh we're kids of the King too!"

"A few people say that," reported Rebecca, "but some are pretty weird. One guy said 'kid of the King, who's that, Elvis Presley?'" We groaned.

After eight weeks Rebecca resumed her University studies. Defying all odds she received her Bachelor's degree and is now in graduate school. There have been more hospitalizations and a second bout with the respirator, but God is great and each day is a miracle. No one who has met Rebecca will ever forget her or the God she so joyfully serves!

Nothing I've experienced compares to what Rebecca goes through every day. She is the supreme example of perseverance. She never gives up! And I'm reminded again how perseverance shaped my life, even my beginnings as "the chosen child."

2

My parents called me "the chosen child" from the time I could sit still long enough to hear a story. Why would I doubt it? Adopted right from the hospital, I was their beautiful blond baby with blue button eyes. Of course I was the only one in the nursery who didn't cry!

Innumerable baby pictures and movies documented their thrill to have me as their daughter. My mother even wrote the story of my first year. Bound in a handsome wooden cover, "When I first arrived on this place called earth...", was my favorite reading. It wasn't until I was a mother myself that I learned of the secretive circumstances of my birth.

As an only child, I enjoyed a family filled with aunts and uncles. The warm and affectionate relationships I had with them helped me to grow up feeling loved and secure. I always felt special, never abandoned. Besides, any curiosity I might have had concerning my biological roots was stifled at a young age.

Occasionally my small childish voice risked, "Mommy, tell me about how I was born?"

The tears in her eyes and the slightly detectable shudder that resonated throughout her body, taught me not to ask very often. "Having a baby makes you sick as a dog. I was lucky to *adopt* you instead. I didn't have to go through all of that."

How remarkable that *I* ever decided to experience pregnancy! But it wasn't until my adopted mom's death that I found the letters of commendation she had received. Then I realized the magnitude of her sacrifice. She forfeited a career she loved in order to raise me.

"Mrs. Murray held the important position of confidential secretary to the Manager, in which capacity she proved herself highly efficient, resourceful, conscientious and loyal to the interest of the company."

Mom told me my birth mother died in child birth, and my birth father was sent to fight overseas in World War II. And when I took piano lessons, she said I was just like him!

"Your Father played the piano Jeannie. He had long fingers that could reach ten keys. He played beautifully." Her words washed over me like warm sunshine. Could I possibly play like him someday? I believed *everything*. It all seemed strangely glamorous to me.

My beginning was definitely different from the lives of my friends - and it has continued that way! I learned at a young age to persevere. That quality followed me into every aspect of my life.

The label I've worn throughout my life developed into much more for me than a term or definition. As a young child, I felt that being *adopted* made me special...I was the chosen one. I had a sense of pride and excitement in the unique way I had become a member of my family! Not until my adult years did I begin to realize the important role both adoption and persevering played in God's plan for my life.

3

What started out for my parents as a festive party lifestyle of the '40's, inched over the line to solitary and secretive drinking. Then my dad's ninety-year-old mother moved in with us which didn't help our already strained family. Grandmother had a regal air about her, and carefully maintained her distinctive Scottish brogue. Years before she had clearly informed my mother, "I didn't raise my son to get married. I raised my son to take care of me!"

And he did.

The cow bell on her nightstand clanged day and night whenever she needed real or imagined help. Many nights Dad made his bed on the living room couch and nursed a little brandy to help restore his interrupted sleep pattern. His fatigue and my mother's resentment fueled their thirst.

In contrast to my mother's private nature, I found it unbearable and impossible for *me* to keep secrets of any kind. Although words were unspoken, my friends and neighbors understood the alcoholism and what was happening in my home.

"Mom, you may think they don't know, but I know they *do*! People aren't stupid!" I was relieved not to have to keep "the secret."

Although I felt loved, I still longed for a family life that more closely resembled that of my friends. Disappointed and hurt by the broken promises of sobriety and normalcy, I tried to get guidance for them.

With my teeth set and my body taut with determination, I waited to see the doctor. How I hoped Dr. Fien would provide the avenue I needed to assist my parents. Finally ushered into an examining room, my resolve quickly turned to fear as I noticed the posted fee schedule. How could I ever pay the thirty dollar consultation fee? Babysitting at forty cents an hour didn't afford such extravagances. Stifling my urge to bolt through the door, I waited. As soon as the doctor entered the small sterile room, I blurted out my concerns.

"My parents can't go on like this. They're ruining their lives... and mine! Isn't there something you can do? They need help."

"You've probably heard this before, Jeannie. But there isn't anything I can do until *they want* help. No one can help them until they decide to help themselves." As I slumped with disappointment, he continued, "I encourage you to take care of yourself. Get good grades. Go to college. You only have a couple of years to go. Help yourself to overcome this."

I drew strength from his words of confidence. It felt good that he believed in me. As I began to stammer about the fee, he finally said, "There will be no charge today." Although my parents continued their same patterns, the visit to Dr. Fien strengthened my resolve. I intended not only to survive, but to overcome *their* problem in *my* life.

* * * * *

I went into the "survival mode," wanting to go to college and have a good life beyond the grasp of my family. Closing the door behind him, my school counselor was insistent.

"Jeannie, you have good grades and high test scores. There is no reason in the world for you not to apply to a University of California school. Don't sell yourself short. You're a responsible student. And you're a leader."

Challenged by his encouragement, I still wondered how this difficult and unhappy time of my life would be used. Would it strengthen me and make me different than I would have been otherwise? Although I didn't really know his word or how to have a relationship with him, I cried out to God. And I stayed involved in my church. My parents praised my responsibleness. But I envied my friends and longed for a mom and dad who waited up to hear about my dates and who would ground me if I wasn't home at midnight. But with my parents often in an alcohol-assisted sound sleep, I made my own rules.

Seeing my mother under alcohol's influence was especially painful and heartbreaking for me. I shed buckets of tears during my teen years and begged her to stop drinking. I was alternately nice and nasty; any ploy that might work. I poured fifths of bourbon down the sink and endured pitchers of "funny tasting" orange juice in our refrigerator.

Tearfully, I confronted her with the bottles of gin I discovered in the laundry hamper. Nothing that I did seemed to help or change things. Ever hopeful, I looked forward to holiday celebrations.

Sterling silver and gold rimmed china graced the table in the living room eating area. But my excitement inevitably turned to despair while every slurred word and stumbled step caused my stomach to churn. Retreating in tears, I ate most of these special dinners alone in my room. As a typical teenager, my room became a refuge for me.

4

I met Neal Satre at a summer wedding during a sweltering 103 degree heat wave. Arriving at the lavish poolside reception, I spotted a circle of my former classmates. I hurried to reunite with friends I hadn't seen since leaving for college the year before. I boldly approached the group and promptly splashed champagne all over Neal's shoes. Grateful for the cooling effect, he slid his arm around the cummerbunded waist of my black and white Lanz. It shocked us both as, in jest, we simultaneously announced, "*Our* wedding is going to be short!" It would be a purposeful contrast to the long and *hot* ceremony we had just experienced.

Neal's blond good looks, his tall frame and his smokey green eyes caught me slightly off balance. I recognized him as the intelligent, talented basketball star and scholarship winner. He was two years ahead of me in high school, but we'd never really been introduced. Suddenly he blurted, "We can have a party at my house." That night we instantly fell in love!

Nine months later, on a perfect spring day, we headed out to celebrate the anniversary of our meeting...nine whole months! The narrow ribbon of mountain road twisted out in front of us. And each rise in elevation challenged Neal's light blue '51 Chevy with the hood wired shut. A fragrant stand of lupine and tender grass provided the ideal picnic spot with the verdant green foothills and Diablo Valley stretching out in the distance. Our frequent dates had created a warm and comfortable togetherness. While devouring the last of the fried chicken I'd prepared, Neal astonished me, "Will you marry me?" The timing was so premature in relation to our college careers that it startled me.

Neal was fun and sensitive *and he was interested in me*! He listened and respected what I had to say. He also shared my background as a child of an alcoholic and understood me and my chaotic family situation.

From that time on, I couldn't imagine marrying anyone else!

A warm embrace and berry-sweet kisses sealed our intentions. We were engaged on April Fool's Day, a date we still celebrate. But there was nothing "foolish" about our commitment. We shopped for the perfect small diamond that would signify our "perfect love." Elated and giddy with enthusiasm, we celebrated our new life together with a romantic dinner at Nikko Sukiyaki.

We planned a long engagement but instead were married only five months later! My Dad seemed serious as he entered my room. "Jeannie, we think you are too young to get married, but Mom and I have decided that we'll support you in whatever you and Neal decide." His words meant a lot to me.

Fran, Neal's Mom, would be the perfect mother-in-law. We actually resembled each other and I loved her words, "You really hit the jackpot with Jeannie, Neal." The festive bridal luncheon she held in my honor made me feel special.

My neighbor, Muriel, helped me with the plans. "I've got just the place for your wedding night! The Alta Mira in Sausalito! It's an old hotel perched on the side of a hill and has a beautiful view of the bay. It's so-o-o romantic. You have to go there!"

Sounded great to me.

Conveniently, the florist lived next door, "I've got to have daisies…white for me and yellow for the bridesmaids. I hope it won't be too hot for them." Tom, the photographer, was my boss at my first high school job at The Camera Shop.

As we always promised, Barbara would be my maid-of-honor, and Neal's brother Dale fell in line as his best man. Eight special friends rounded out the wedding party.

As our wedding day neared, I dreaded the possibility of embarrassment and earnestly prayed my parents could keep from drinking for just one day. The sherbet punch and coffee at the church hall reception would surely help. A champagne colored brocade suit assisted in redeeming some of my mother's former attractiveness and, not to be outdone, my Dad donned a fashionable white dinner jacket to walk me down the aisle.

Our church wedding was a small ceremony with many friends in attendance. Slender white tapers flickered on the altar and white bows and greenery bordered the wooden pews. Although my wedding dress belonged to Jo Anne and my veil was borrowed, I felt as beautiful as any bride! And, for once, my parents didn't disappoint me. Dashing to our car in a shower of rice, we laughed at "Just Married" sprayed in shaving cream on our rear window. The dozens of cans hitched to our bumper gave us a clamorous and festive send off.

Eleven p.m. in Sausalito wasn't exactly conducive to an elegant wedding meal. "The only place I can suggest is Juanita's Galley," the bellman volunteered. It's an old ferry boat down the road. You can't miss it. At least you can get a steak sandwich and they serve pretty late."

Taking his hint, we approached Juanita's. Seeing the run-down hulk gave me a clue that we were way over dressed. "This hat's staying in the car," I announced as I tossed my black velveteen pillbox onto the back seat. As we neared the glass door I unpinned my catalaya orchid corsage, "The flowers go too!" Feeling like conspicuous honeymooner's we quietly entered the converted boat.

"Whatcha kids want?" bellowed the huge muu-muu clad figure behind the counter. Could it be Juanita herself?

"A couple of steak sandwiches would be good...ah, to go." While we waited we carefully observed our surroundings...Christmas lights in September, sawdust strewn on the slanting floor, decorations of every imaginable kind hanging everywhere, and a live rooster prancing around the bar.

"Okay, here's your food." We grabbed it and ran.

"Oh, I'm so glad to get out of there. Here we are in our going away suits. Didn't you feel like a dope?" We broke up in fits of laughter as we headed for the hotel. Our beautiful room provided us with a backdrop of sparkling city lights. The bouquet of my favorite flowers, chilled champagne, and our sandwiches from Juanita's provided a special wedding feast.

It wasn't a very practical time to be married with my two years of college to finish and Neal just starting four years of Dental School. But we were full of optimism and excitement regarding our life and future together.

5

We settled into our first apartment, a studio where we had to walk through the closet to get to the bathroom. Living on only fifty dollars a month from each of our parents, plus what we earned during vacations caused us no anxiety at all. Our new life together was glorious and we both had the single-minded purpose of graduation.

Much of our entertainment as married students consisted of watching ships meander under the Golden Gate. A bluff high above the water provided us with a panoramic view of where San Francisco Bay merges with the swirling tides of the Pacific Ocean. We accomplished hours of leisurely study in the warmth of our English Ford mini wagon. Enjoying California's sunset and munching enchiladas from the "Hot House" at the beach concluded our idea of a perfect day.

Watching people from our city window took the place of TV for us. People from the shift change at U.C. Medical Center racing to their cars or waiting for the "N Judah" created a true life scenario. With great rattling and sparks flying, the street car disconnections at Carl and Irving were hard to ignore. And the blazing lights of tow trucks were a common sight on our steep Arguello hill. Still, the most amusing days were when the '49ers played at Kezar Stadium. Our neighbors sold parking in their driveways to desperate fans and a sense of excitement punctuated the air. We loved hearing the roar of the crowds. And when the games were over we watched inebriated wanderers try to find their cars. Living in the city was a fun and invigorating experience.

I graduated with an elementary credential and my new teaching job filled me with excitement. Having been hired on my first interview gave me the confidence I needed. The faculty at Pacific Heights School was young and energetic and our creative zeal was appreciated. I loved my first graders...and they loved me back! And their parents were thrilled that *I'd* taught their children to read! I felt responsible in a favorable way and like part of a team - Neal and me. It was a great feeling!

After two years of teaching, it was now Neal's turn and Graduation Day was exhilarating. Even Neal's scholarly cap and gown couldn't conceal his boyish enthusiasm.

But despite the celebration, the Viet Nam War loomed over graduation. "Neal, what if you set up a practice and get drafted? There's a good chance you know. How awful to get stuck with a big bank loan." Neal's step-father's counsel seemed sound. So along with many of his classmates, Neal joined the Army.

"Medical Field Service School" at Fort Sam Houston sounded challenging! Life was a continuing adventure set out before us, and our eyes lit up with every bend in the road approaching the city.

"Neal, I love Ft. Sam! Not working, a furnished apartment, a pool, a salary! This is living!" Instant friends doing the same month on duty made it a congenial scene. "Tomorrow I'm going to 'Officer's Wives School.' Guess I'll learn about calling cards and hats. They always have something to keep us busy, otherwise it's pool and tan time! Oh, and we've got to hit the PX again. They have the best bargains!"

Other things impressed Neal. "Texas sure has huge clouds and thunderstorms. Can you believe it? That lightening bolt cracked the tree right out in our parking lot last night. Wait'll you see it! No wonder it was so loud. It sure is different from living in San Francisco."

6:00 a.m. came early on graduation day. Groggy, but excited, we rushed to prepare for this last function at Fort Sam Houston. Neal struck a handsome figure in his dress blues as he fell into line with the other Dental and Medical officers assembled on the parade grounds. The impressive ceremony culminated with their commissioning as "Captains."

With some dentists and most of the physicians receiving orders for Viet Nam, we were happy to be going to the Midwest. We felt protected from overseas duty while serving in Ft. Leavenworth, Kansas. As the home of the "Command and General Staff College of the Army," an educational facility, there were no troops to send.

The Sergeant in the olive drab sedan led us to our Rose Street address in town. With no room on post, they rented a little house for us and we were expectant. An expansive front porch framed the rural two-bedroom bungalow set on a shady cul-de-sac. And a tiny basement room was pointed out as "the place to hide during a tornado watch."

Those tornado instructions and the slow pace of the small town provided a stark contrast to our more familiar San Francisco city life. Guitar playing neighbors, Pearl and Dutch, even had an "out house!" We felt like we'd entered "the twilight zone!" And our Christmas card... a photo of Neal and me in the famous Grant Wood, couple-with-the-pitch-fork pose reflected our experience. But with friendly neighbors and a fun group of dental friends, we enthusiastically embarked on our new mid-west adventure.

6

Shortly after arriving in Kansas, nausea overtook me and a simple lab test confirmed our hopeful suspicion. "It's seemed so long. I can't believe it's happening, can you? Six months of disappointment. But now it's real! Can you believe that *we're* going to have a baby??" Neal was giddy too.

At my three month appointment the first news came, "There might be two in there. Or there could be a problem. I'm having trouble hearing a heartbeat, but I'm not worried. We'll wait and take x-rays later." Then, "Lose ten pounds and come back in two weeks." And he left me lying on the table. I changed doctors!

X-rays at seven months revealed an undeniable picture. "Yep, there are two in there! A boy and a girl," Bellowed the young technician.

"No, I can't really tell, but *there are two*. Come, look and see for yourself." The black and white film displayed two babies traversing my hugely expanded belly! I couldn't wait to tell Neal.

Then as my blood pressure peaked, the doctor worried about toxemia, common in a first pregnancy with twins. Hospitalization seemed imminent. Going to the hospital so early was disappointing, but concern for our babies ultimately prevailed. Feigning bravado, I greeted Neal's lunch time visit with a pink bow in my hair. But soon, my forced cheerfulness was irreparably shattered.

Neal entered my private room accompanied by a nurse. I'd never seen him look so pale. Then he blurted out his inconceivable news. "Jeannie, I have orders for Viet Nam." My heart sank as numbness overwhelmed me. Willing away the tears that stung my eyes, we silently clung to one another for support.

Later I started to construct some practical plans for me and my babies. And I realized I would soon have *two* to care for...by myself! So I began to chart my options. Return to California or stay in Kansas? My biggest concern was for the well-being of the babies that stretched and churned inside of me. There was no ignoring their presence and my discomfort grew along with them!

The "few days" in the hospital stretched on to a month. Away from friends and family, I found it was one of the most frustrating times of my life. To make matters worse, only family members could visit the maternity ward. What a way to spend our last days together before Neal's departure to a war zone!

"Twins are usually three to five weeks early. You should plan on three weeks early and we're hoping to get them to five pounds." Trusting the doctor's predictions, we sent our furniture to California and I marked time in the maternity ward.

Thank goodness for Carol, my only hospital friend. Hospitalized with a complication in her pregnancy, she kept me company. Every morning we shuffled down to the nursery to see the babies born during the night. Later, as longtime residents, we even folded hospital laundry.

Finally my water broke during the night and by the next afternoon the contractions came. Neal frantically rushed in from the Dental Clinic just in time to console me.

"We'll give you a cervical block, but that's all you can have. You're going to need to push. But we'll have the anesthesiologist on hand to put you out for the second one. The second twin is often breech." The doctor's words jolted me with reality. This would prove to be an eventful ordeal! As the shots took hold I happily felt my labor pains subside. Glaring lights glinted off the sterile tile walls and steel surgical equipment. Transferring me to the delivery table wasn't an easy task and I've never felt less graceful. But how grateful I was that Neal, as part of the Medical/Dental Corps, was allowed to join me in the delivery room.

"If you're going to faint, lean against the wall and slide down. We don't want you to fall on her," were the doctor's only instructions.

Reluctant to threaten my feeling of strength and wellbeing, I declined the nurse's offer of a mirror. The doctors kept up a running banter, "Gee, I wish we could hurry this up. I'm missing the football game."

"I haven't had dinner yet. Have you?"

Somehow their humor didn't phase me. Neal cheered me on, "Come on Babe, you can do it! Keep pushing. You're doing great. Just a little more."

I pushed and *pushed* with determination to finally deliver Douglas *breech*! Derek slid right out eight minutes later – 7lbs. and 7lbs. 9ozs., both 21 ins. long, and nine days late! No wonder I was able to balance a coffee cup on my pregnant belly. With black eyebrows, thick eyelashes and crowns of black hair, they didn't look at all like the blond or bald babies I had expected.

The boys had a great start in life, but their size took a toll on my body. I was so exhausted that I hardly noticed I hadn't even held my babies. The nurse tucked me in for the night and I fell immediately asleep.

The shrill ring of the phone pierced Neal's much needed rest. Tempted to roll over and ignore the irritation, he stumbled to the kitchen. The stern voice on the other end quickly jolted him out of his sleepy daze. "Captain Satre, this is Captain Graf. Your wife has had some unexpected bleeding during the night and she needs a transfusion. Her condition seems serious." Neal fumbled with his clothes as he raced to the VW. Shoelaces could wait. The few blocks to Munson Army Hospital seemed to stretch to miles. Bounding into my room, he found me pale and sleepy against Army issued white sheets. He could only watch, wait.... and even though we didn't know Jesus in a personal way, he *prayed*.

Instead of greeting my babies with cuddles and love, I was *sick* and content to sleep unaware of the hectic activity pulsing around me. I occasionally wondered, *"Neal, why aren't you at work? What are you doing? Why are you sitting by my bed all day?"* While Neal watched over me, he also pondered how he would care for twin babies...alone. The joyous time of childbirth had suddenly become extremely stressful.

Watching me shake violently from the allergic reaction to the blood transfusion meant to strengthen me, he wondered, *"How could this be happening after such a healthy pregnancy and great delivery?"* It seemed unfair. *"What can I do with two babies and no Mom?"* Unanswered questions flooded Neal's mind. My slow recovery continued to delay that first moment when I would hold Derek and Douglas in my arms.

Neal became a fixture at the nursery window admiring his handsome new sons. Proudly, he pointed out to anyone who would listen, "See those twin babies? They're my sons! Aren't they fantastic?"

"That's nothing! I delivered twelve last night," the Army veterinarian piped up. "Twelve baby pigs!"

"How insulting!" Neal looked chagrined. "Why would anyone compare my boys with *pigs*?" Neal was earnest as he related the story.

When our sons were ten days old the three of us finally came home from the hospital. Everyone on the Army Post welcomed Neal as the "Father of the New Twins." But no one had even *seen* me! But no wonder! It had been quite some time since I had been in the mainstream of life.

7

According to the "instruction manual," we needed a handcrafted nursery. Instead, we came home to a nearly empty house. We had sent the furniture to the California apartment my Dad had rented for me and the boys. Only our king-sized bed, two portable bassinets, a changing table, and director's chairs borrowed from neighbors remained. What a contrast to what the "manual" said was required for twins. With Neal's total involvement, we handled the changing and feeding routine night and day. He would diaper and I would feed.

However, my first extended time alone with the babies left me extremely anxious. Everything was fine until they decided it was time for lunch. While they both screamed in hunger, I fumbled with formula and plastic baggies, bottles and nipples, baby state-of-the-art in 1967. When Neal got home we were back to four hands instead of two.

"I don't know how I'll ever do this without you. I can't even do it now and you're here," I wailed. Dreading the day Neal would leave, I knew I would be in charge alone.

We felt like VIP's when the Army chauffeur whisked us to Kansas City for our flight to San Francisco. Both of us held a baby and hefted diaper bags and bottles. Tucked in their little airline box beds, the boys slept peacefully as we winged our way west. After arriving back in California we unpacked boxes and enjoyed being a family for five short days. Then it was time for Neal to leave.

We went to our favorite classic Italian restaurant where the waiters sang, just because they wanted to, where memories had been made during our four years of city living. The famous San Francisco sourdough French bread that we bought frozen in gourmet shops while living in the Midwest, now reminded us that we were back home. This wonderful evening preceded and eased our dreaded good-bye.

During that year, the boys and I survived. But it wasn't until several years later that I knew that it was *God* who deserved the credit for how well we managed. Bonnie and Ron, great next door neighbors, became our close friends. Their daughter, Kellene, was eight months older than the boys and we had a grand time together.

Throwing both strollers into my red VW, we often headed for the mall. Nothing stopped us! Bonnie saved us many times and she always showed up at the right moment, "Do I hear a baby crying?" Then she'd grab the "culprit" and head for the rocking chair. She fed me dinners and Ron fixed my car. Their friendship helped fend off the loneliness of that Viet Nam year.

Then there was Mrs. Spencer, the grandmotherly widow who enjoyed babysitting and became "Nana" to the boys. Their support gave me the encouragement I needed.

Not wanting Neal to feel left out, I packed up an artificial Christmas tree and homemade ornaments that arrived in crumbs. But preparing them was therapy for me. Attempting to develop his close relationship to the boys, I mailed piles of baby photos and even audio tapes of Derek and Douglas crying during the night. "Its 3 a.m., the boys are screaming and I can hear Mr. Lincoln flipping over in his bed in the apartment upstairs! Someone told me that persistence is a sign of intelligence. These guys must score off the charts!" In exchange, Neal's many letters encouraged me.

> "You poor, exhausted, overworked and underpaid baby. I'm sure the little talk with Dr. Davis gave you some good advice. It would be easy to let the kids dominate your life and naturally you don't want that

to happen. But as you point out, you are outnum-
bered - tch! You don't have much choice but to suffer
right through those miserable 'sick' nights, Toots. It
won't be long before I'll be able to suffer right along
with you. So don't throw in the towel. I can only
hope that you haven't caught the stomach flu - but
it will always be something - right?"

Having sole responsibility for two babies definitely made
it a challenging year for me. How I yearned for Neal's presence and support. My days, filled with bathing, changing,
feeding, walks, laundry and nap schedules, flew by. But seeing families spending time together on the weekends seared
my heart. It was an unnecessary reminder of how desperately
I missed my husband.

His life wasn't a picnic either. Danger preceded as he
was shuffled several times to different landing zones throughout Viet Nam. We corresponded daily and I often found his
news disconcerting. "I've been getting some flying in. Sometimes the Forward Air Control pilots let me go up with them.
I'm taking the greatest pictures!" I was beside myself when I
learned that "FAC" planes are tiny cessnas that go before the
bombing strikes!

"Don't you realize that you're a father now! Please Neal,
don't take any chances that you don't have to."

During the first Tet Offensive I received grievous news
from Neal. "Our Lt. Col. is looking for a promotion. He wants
to say that we're providing dental care for the troops at the
DMZ. We're leaving by convoy tomorrow."

Seeing the casualties on the evening news deepened my
concern. But, as always, Neal stayed pretty matter-of-fact.

"Well, we arrived safely, but it's really a mess. There's
no place for us. The Marines seem to be pretty annoyed having a bunch of dumb dentists running

around with 45's. We're just digging bunkers and filling sand bags. I'm sleeping in a bunker with some pretty good sized rats."

The prospect of a Hawaii R&R kept me going! But we were advised to wait until near the end of the tour to see each other. Knowing he'd soon be home might make our second parting easier. So I sewed summer shifts and shopped for sandals for our island rendezvous. Friends expected that Neal would want to see the boys, but he wanted *me*...all to himself! And I longed for the respite.

Deciding to pursue a new "look," I headed for the beauty parlor. Although my fashionable Sasson cut trimmed away my blond highlights, it gave me a psychological lift. But when I landed in Honolulu, Neal looked right past me. Grabbing his arm, I pulled him close. "Good grief, I didn't even recognize you! What did you do to your hair?"

Neal looked good and healthy but thin. Hawaii was a beautiful setting to renew our relationship. Our eighth floor picture window framed Diamond Head, Waikiki and sunny blue skies. Seven extraordinary days filled with walks on the beach and tropical salads were occasionally interrupted by visits to Tripler Army hospital. Dysentery was a common problem with the soldiers, but nothing could dampen the joy of being together again. It was like we had never been away.

However, the inevitable good-bye was grueling. Hundreds of forlorn G.I.'s formed an unending line that snaked around the tarmac. Uniformly skinny frames and close cropped crew cuts gave them all a boyish vulnerable look. Teen-aged brides, infant children and their grandmothers completed the sorrowful picture. Tearful embraces, shaking sobs and quiet good-byes filled the airport. Many of these young men; mine sweepers, artillery soldiers, and field hospital medics, would never come home. It was a gripping scene that I'll never forget. Feigning a brave front, Neal and I tried to be cool. Sunglasses shielded the pain we felt as we savored our final embrace.

The flight home left me feeling lonely and pensive. Facing a second adjustment to life alone seemed insufferable. So I relived our Hawaiian reunion and counted the ninety-plus days until we could be together for good.

It is now clear that God, in His love for us, had His hand in our circumstances. But how much richer our lives could have been if we had only known to call on Him and the real strength that He offers. Now I have experienced how God hears and answers prayers in real ways. He continues to provide people to help and encourage me and fills me with a sense of peace even when the circumstances aren't peaceful. His love for me is beyond my understanding. I regret having missed those opportunities to depend on Him when I needed Him most. But the character and confidence both Neal and I developed during that year prepared us for many more challenges and adversities yet to come.

8

Neal's Med. Evac flight from Viet Nam arrived at Travis Air Force Base on August 11, 1968, just in time for Derek and Douglas' first birthday. But his call caught me by surprise.

"Jeannie? Hi, it's me!"

My Dad, enjoying a period of sobriety, stayed with the sleeping boys. Dropping the ironing, I ripped out my curlers and headed our VW toward Fairfield, California. The car strained as I forced the accelerator beyond it's capability. Spotting Neal alone at the curb, I screeched to a stop. What a fabulous sight! I hoped our hugs and kisses would never end! But what a job it was to squeeze his foot locker and two crates into our tiny car.

Before the door was even closed, Neal breathlessly began relating his harrowing flight. "I got a Med Evac flight out of DaNang. As soon as we took off, I learned that the flight was terminating in Japan. I couldn't imagine what I'd do there. How I'd get home. *Then* a flight attendant came to me and said, 'Captain? There's a G.I. with multiple body wounds who's getting air sick. His jaw is wired shut. We need your help!'"

"I told her, 'You don't understand, I'm a *dentist.*'"

"'I'm sorry sir, but you are the ranking medical officer on board.'"

"The poor guy was really miserable. I cut the wires on his mouth, so that helped. Then we landed in Japan, and I got off the plane wondering what to do next. The Air Force medical officer who met us was *Steve Chandler*! Remember, I played basketball with him in Berkeley? I was so glad to see someone I knew! He said I could come home with him. But then Steve got me right on a flight to Travis."

Finally at our apartment, we peered at the babies snuggled in their cribs. Derek's slight stirring served as an excuse to pick him up. Such a gorgeous warm little bundle in his aqua terry cloth sleepers. "Look Derek, it's Daddy," I whispered. "Do you want to see Daddy? Gently, I moved closer to Neal. Derek's saucer blue eyes opened wide as he decidedly shook his head, "No, n-o-o." Fortunately, Neal handled this initial rejection with understanding.

Wrapped in Neal's strong arms, I felt assured that he was actually home. Now I could relax. I languished in the joy I experienced being together after such a *long* year!

"What does Neal think of his boys?" became the common question.

"Jeannie, help. Come quick!" Neal hollered from the kitchen. Expecting disaster, I found Neal off balance with one knee attempting to block the open frig. Just trying to get the orange juice, he seemed frantically embroiled in a full scale battle with four little hands frantically grasping anything in reach. "They follow me everywhere...even to the bathroom!" Did he *really* think this was news to me?

The early morning crash from the boys' bedroom reverberated through our modest apartment. "What's happened now?' gasped Neal as he dashed from our room. Wedged between the diaper pail and the toppled six drawer dresser we found a panicked and scantily diapered Douglas screaming his head off. Rushing to help I saw the open drawers he'd climbed! Only the tall plastic pail had saved him from serious injury or death!

"The boys are great, but I'm not used to them," Neal confessed breathlessly, as he screwed the dresser to the wall. The little collage booklet I made and sent to Neal in Viet Nam proved to be more prophetic than I realized:

"Changing us? Impossible!
Dressing us? A chore!
Feeding us? Somewhat a mess!
We're always anxious to explore.
We laugh out loud. We 'Da-da-da'
And often times we fuss.
We're ready for you Dad......
But are YOU ready for US??"

What a change from the time when we were just a couple going to school and living in our studio.

Derek and Douglas were typical toddlers, weaving and often tumbling as they learned to walk. "Neal help them!"

"They're O.K. They're doing just fine. They can handle it," was his casual reply.

"Boy, Neal has a lot to learn!" I told myself. So one morning when my favorite child psychologist, Dr. Heim Gniott, was on TV I was anxious for Neal to listen, and I urged him to watch and become educated.

"The father's primary role in child rearing is to protect the child from the mother's over protectiveness!" A self-satisfied grin swept across Neal's face as I quickly reached for the television's "off" button. You can be sure we still talk about *that* statement! But like so many other couples, we often seem to balance one another by our different temperaments and parenting styles.

9

Shortly after Neal arrived home, we bought our first house. Through the process of elimination we settled on a ranch style house on a corner lot in a rural neighborhood. At the time we never dreamed of the expanded version that would gradually evolve over the next twenty years.

I was happy with my choice to stay home to be a wife and a mother. My experience as an elementary school teacher helped me teach my boys and I enjoyed digging into craft and holiday projects with them. But a feeling of restlessness was setting in.

"Isn't there something more to life than housework? Do we just go through these motions of living to grow old and die?"

Busy with his new dental practice, Neal didn't share my concern.

But being at home with young children had its own sense of isolation. The time was the early '70's and I began questioning all of the things my generation had expected to make us happy...two cars, a home in the suburbs.... I had achieved my goals: a college education, a job I enjoyed, a wonderful husband and two handsome children. That's where *my* goals had stopped which was not unusual for women my age. I should have been happy. Instead I felt an unexplainable emptiness.

So I began reading current psychology, I joined a humanistic group and I even had my own idea about what God thought - "the gospel according to Jeannie!" Although my life and marriage were happy, none of these avenues provided the meaning and fulfillment I was looking for. Then I read a book where the psychologist related the story of a humble cleaning woman who had touched the lives of many people. When she grew old, she could look back at her life and see the difference that she had made. I decided that I wanted my life to count for something! Derek and Douglas were nearing kindergarten and up to this point all I had wanted to do was play tennis, take an art class and have a few minutes to myself. More than twenty-five years later these things still sound pretty good to me!

During this same time, Neal and I discussed having a third child. So when the boys were three years old, the time seemed right and we became enchanted with the idea of having a daughter. We didn't want more twins! One "set" per family was entirely enough. And, since the boys are fraternal, we had a good chance of having a second set. Two thoughts tugged at my heart. Why *have* another baby when there are children already born who are without families? Also Ehrlichman's *Population Bomb* was on the best seller list. His notion that no responsible family should have more than two children was a serious issue to us.

My own adoption also fueled my desire to reach out to a homeless child. After all, my family had taken a chance on me, so I wanted to help another child. And, although I was willing, Neal wasn't eager to repeat the harrowing childbirth scene, so adoption appealed to him as well. But my inquiries to our local agencies garnered negative responses.

"I'm sorry but we have no children available for people who can have children and who already have two children."

We both felt discouraged.

As Toddy and I approached the country club drive I wondered aloud about the "mother of nine" who was billed as our luncheon speaker. "Why isn't she home doing the laundry? Can you just imagine nine kids? I can hardly handle two!"

I was awestruck as blond, vibrant Dorothy Atwood Debolt stepped to the lectern. As she related the poignant story of her children, several of whom were adopted internationally, I immediately felt drawn in. We could do this too!

Although inspired by her enthusiasm, good looks and compassion, there was no way I could have predicted the large role that she and her family would play in our lives in the future.

But would Neal share my excitement for inter-country adoption? Armed with the Holt Adoption brochure passed out at the luncheon, I anxiously approached him. How could he resist the sad little Asian face and their motto "Every Child Deserves a Home of His Own?" While enthusiastically relating Dorothy's whole story, his favorable response surprised me. "That sounds interesting. Why don't you write to them and find out more about it?"

International adoption was uncommon in the '70's, so we had no idea what to expect. But seeing so many desperate orphans in Viet Nam opened Neal's heart to the needs of homeless children. We were thrilled and amazed to quickly receive Holt's response to my letter: "We do have some older and handicapped children, but right now our need is homes for infants to a year old." What a perfect match we thought!

10

We had always dreamed of a girl – a little sister for Derek and Douglas and a daughter for us. After an agonizing and extended period of soul searching, we finally felt ready to apply for our home study. Nervously, I dialed the State of California Department of Social Services. My enthusiasm was immediately dashed by what I heard. The social worker, trained in inter-country adoption, treated me as if I were brainless! Ticking off every possible road block to adoption, he acted as if we had never thought of them!

"Why do you want to adopt a child of another race? Don't you know that the children are found on the street? They could be sick. What about your other children?" A barrage of unexpected negativism flowed through my receiver.

Tears covered my cheeks as I struggled for control. Why such a rude and uncaring attitude? If only I could confront him face to face. Embarrassed by my outburst, I abruptly ended the conversation. I was relieved that he didn't know my name. Could he become our social worker?

We had considered all of the questions. The racial issue seemed important. But Neal was right, "Jeannie, people's lives are so hectic and complex. They won't spend much time worrying about what we're doing. They'll either say 'Why are you doing it?' 'That's nice for them, but I'd never do it.' 'How great, I wish I could do it too.' Then they'll go back to living their own busy lives. We have to decide what's right for us and go with it."

We were comfortable with our conscientious decision. Our sense of purpose was impenetrable.

So we approached our parents. My blind and frail mother smiled her benign approval but Dad seemed more concerned. "Jeannie, you can't save the world. This is just one child." How relieved I was that they didn't even mention race. I knew they could accept our new daughter as one of their own. Besides, having adopted me, adoption wasn't a new concept.

Neal's Mom, Fran, was ecstatic. "I think it's just wonderful! I wish I could have done the same thing. I can't wait to see her." John, Neal's stepfather, worried us. How would he react to our news? Since he called Derek and Douglas "Boy," we figured it couldn't get much worse. His Okay both surprised and relieved us.

With our application to the Holt Adoption Agency in the mail, a long wait ensued. When could California start the home study? There would be several meetings, Neal and I together plus each of us alone. It sounded a bit like psychological therapy to me.

Anxiously, I readjusted the coffee and cookies that I had artfully arranged to impress our social worker. While waiting I bombarded Neal with my insecurities, "Will she like us? Is the house clean enough? Do we make enough money? What if she *doesn't* like us?"

Typically, his steady demeanor balanced my "what if" projections. Neal didn't feel threatened by social workers but enjoyed seeing my excitement and nervous enthusiasm. His loving encouragement calmed me, "Jeannie, we have so much to offer. What's not to like? Relax!"

I greeted Ms. Cray before she could even reach the house. Straining under the load of her bulging brief case she slowly approached our front steps. I fought to bridle my impatience. Knowing I would be grilled on my entire life, I harbored no secrets. I was eager to share my life as a wife, mother and woman. Neal, on the other hand, saw it as a hurdle to get through. He didn't feel led to offer more information than was asked of him. Instead, our minds became boggled with talk of fingerprints, immigration forms, medical exams and recommendations. Official looking documents littered our couch.

Finally, Ms. Cray got personal. With enthusiasm, I volunteered answers before her questions were even formed. We were grilled on our motives. "Why do you feel the *need* for more children when you already have two healthy boys?" she chided.

"*Oh boy, we're in trouble now!*" I thought. "*Is loving a child and giving them a home not acceptable? Wait until she hears that I'm adopted. She'll really think I'm a basket case.*" Doubt and fear of rejection fleeted through my mind. My facade of strength and confidence disguised my real feelings.

I was taken aback with her, "It's wonderful that you're adopted too. You feel so comfortable with your experience. Your acceptance and positive attitude will be sure to help your child." Her words made my heart sing. Maybe this wouldn't be so bad after all.

"But," she continued, "you know that these children may not be very healthy. Their mothers usually haven't had prenatal or post-natal care and the children are abandoned. Most often they are found on the street. Of course they have to pass a physical before they come to the United States. But the chances are good that your child might not be too bright." Her negative comments were balanced with the vision of the bright happy kids I had heard about. Although Ms. Cray was likeable, a cloud of gloom hovered over our first meeting. We watched her go, our future arbitrarily in her hands.

"Why was she so contrary when we're full of optimism and excitement? Were the children really that sick? Would we be depriving another family of a child when we could still have biological babies?" Again Neal's calm, confident attitude and tender touch countered my questioning. Instead of "weeding us out," our determination deepened.

Knowing other adoptive parents really encouraged us. Seeing their success helped us to "keep at it" even though the whole process was an emotional roller coaster. Clear and sure of what we wanted, we persevered. We felt more confident from then on. Now we were going for it! The DeBolt's saying "No risk, no reward," became our family motto.

11

We were prepared for almost anything, except writing our belief in Christ as part of the application. Even with a "Christian" agency, who would expect to have to explain our faith, or lack of it? Although we knew what they wanted, we weren't really sure who or what we believed. Except for weddings, we hadn't been in a church for ten years!

Frustrated, we wondered how to satisfy guidelines of the agency while not being fully committed to their Godly standards.

According to the information letter,

> "The Christian life is a life of trust in Jesus Christ to save us from our sins, our failures, our mistakes. It is a life of personal relationship with Him by faith.....We go into detail here because we want to make clear the kind of living, vital faith in Christ that we seek in our adoptive homes...This is to help you examine your own all-important relationship to God as well as to help us evaluate how well we fulfill our purpose."

I believed Jesus was a good man and teacher. I even remembered some of what I learned in Sunday school. But now I didn't really understand Him as the Son of God and Savior. Further self-examination began for both Neal and me. Little by little, I developed a hunger for spiritual truth in my life but Neal didn't seem as interested.

At the same time, we thought about Sunday School for Derek and Douglas. "Karen's been telling me about the children's program at her church. It would probably be good training for them."

Pensively, I waited for Neal's input. Although not eager, he was open to the subject. "The boys can choose their religion as adults. But, I guess this would give them a basis for their choice."

"I hated being 'dropped off.' If they go to Sunday school then we'll have to go to church!" I strongly identified with our role as caring parents.

"Whether we believe it or not?" Neal questioned drolly.

Our first visit to church was real culture shock! Where did they find all these men with short hair and *suits* in the '70's? We saw a reactionary group of conservative people and were mildly amused. Comfortable in our anonymity, we warmed the pew in the last row of the huge sanctuary.

My friend Barbara, a Bible student, stirred my interest. "Neal, Barbara says that the world's going to end."

His response, as before, was nonchalant and his attitude was complacent. He was too busy worrying about getting his dental practice started to be concerned with matters of eternity.

Questions gnawed at me, but what about the answers? When the evangelical minister of the church called, I immediately arranged a visit. Apprehension filled his voice, "Now tell your husband, that I won't come over if he doesn't want me to. Whenever he wants me to leave, I'll go right away."

Neal and I laughed. "It sounds like he's had some pretty nerve wracking experiences." We rushed through dinner and baths for the boys, and hoped for their co-operation while we talked.

Punctual and enthusiastic, the minister bounded onto the porch. The two women hanging behind him, calmly balanced his boisterous personality. After some polite chit-chat, he zeroed in on the point, "If you died tonight, would you be let into heaven?"

"Of course! I'm a good wife and mother. I've never hurt anyone. And, after all, I'm even going to rescue the life of a foreign orphan through adoption."

Not impressed, he kept going, explaining things I hadn't remembered. "The Bible teaches that the only way to God is through Jesus who says, 'I am the way the truth and the life. No one comes to the Father except through Me'" (John 14:6). As he continued, another verse grabbed my attention, "For it is by grace you have been saved, through faith—and this not from yourselves, it is the gift of God" (Ephesians 2:8).

A gift? That appealed to me. Although put off by his style, what he said was interesting. None of this was in "the gospel according to Jeannie."

Neal's response was contrary to mine. "I love life! We live in a beautiful place. If I can impart a respect for the world and a love of nature to my boys, I'll feel I've done a good job."

Undeterred, the minister invited us to pray with him. Neal wasn't interested, but I was! Women's lib. was new and I thought, *"Just because you don't want to live forever, doesn't mean that I don't!"* Furtively glancing at Neal, I kneeled in my living room and sincerely repeated the minister's prayer asking Jesus to be my Savior and Lord.

I've never regretted my decision.

"Everything will surely be wonderful after that!" I thought. But I was more confused than ever. My days were filled with frustration and interspersed with tears. *"What will I say to my friends? They show no signs of spiritual interest."* My life had been defined by every current mode of thinking. *"Who am I now?"* I wondered.

Joining a small Bible study sponsored by Christian Women's Club got me on track. Through the patience of the women and the study of God's word, I began to learn the gospel according to God. It was very different from Jeannie's version! I was surprised to see that He often doesn't think the same way I do. The group was bombarded with my constant questioning. "What about the people in Africa? What about evolution? Did Noah really exist?" Wisely, they continued to point me back to Jesus. This began a journey of learning and growing. It was exciting to see how God's plan for my life and the lives of my family members would unfold in surprising ways.

What I found was:

"A man who fits no formula! He is the Man who meets our deepest needs, challenges our inflexibility, calls us to follow Him and fellowship with some unexpected fellow followers. He opens our minds to new ways of thinking, our spirits to new ways of worshiping, our hearts to new ways of loving. He is the God of the unexpected!"[1]

Neal and I have discovered the validity of each of these statements in our lives. We especially understand "the God of the unexpected!"

One of the first things I learned was "love shows itself in action" (1 John 3:18, TEV) That's what we were doing by continuing with the adoption of our first child. By this time, Neal had begun to study the Bible on his own and committed his life to Jesus quietly through prayer. Suddenly, his reading had new and deeper meaning and he was astounded to discover "Even to this day when Moses is read, a veil covers their hearts. But whenever anyone turns to the Lord, the veil is taken away" (2 Corinthians 3:15-16). What a confirmation of his spiritual commitment and experience!

12

Although our adoption started out as a humanitarian act, we later realized how God had directed us. But there were still "down days." Just mothering the boys created stress. I secretly wondered, *"Why were we even considering a third child? How could I handle it? My home life was already demanding."* "Pre-Adoptive Pregnancy," described in Jan de Hartog's book *The Children*, encouraged me:

> "Your opinions of yourself will be subject to the same vacillations. One day, looking at yourself in the mirror, you feel that this is really what you were created for, that you would like not one, but four, six children; you smile as you look at yourself, for you are looking at a true mother, brimming over with love, calm and competence. The next day, the haggard creature in the mirror will be a barren, neurotic female who in a moment of megalomania and frustration has plunged headlong into a commitment for life to a total stranger, a sinister little foundling who may, for all you know, turn out to be another Jack the Ripper, or merely a juvenile delinquent. What in the name of God made you presume that you had any talent, any natural aptitude for rearing a child of Asian parents..."[2]

Inter-country adoption was filled with frustrating periods of waiting. But when "the day" arrived, we quickly forgot our fragmented nerves and severely tested patience.

"Your daughter's picture has arrived! Can we set up a time when I can bring it out to show you? I'd like both you and Neal to be there." Ms. Cray's words made me giddy.

Nothing could have prepared us for that little face. Seeing her for the first time was like long, drawn out child birth. But my labor had been *emotional*! Our hearts immediately went out to this dear baby who looked so distraught. Our baby! "Two month old Kim-Jin-Jung, (Lia Kim Satre to us) was found on the *streets* of Seoul. Her birth date was wrapped in her quilt." An act of love in a desperate situation?

"This isn't uncommon," Ms. Cray reassured us. "The Korean government doesn't allow people to release children for adoption.* They're often found near churches or police stations where help is available for them. Now she's in a foster home." (*This policy has changed)

"Look at our baby!" I quietly gasped. Neal and I zeroed in on the 2"x2" black and white photo like a laser. Months of pent up emotion swelled in both of us. What a picture! Lia's hair stood on end and a remnant of a tear was apparent on her cheek. Little rose bud lips completed the portrait. A brief paragraph concluded the information available to us:

> "The child seems to be good in physical development for her age, appears to be stubborn but will improve if cared for with tender love. She should be placed in a loving family as soon as possible to grow and develop well under good care."

We were ecstatic!

The four of us worked together to arrange a little girl's room. The boys, five years old, sanded the crib and held the ladder while Neal hung the pink and yellow daisy wallpaper. The dotted Swiss wallpaper background gave the room the delicate look so essential to me. The boys were always part of this adoption in a big way!

Every day I raced to the mail box. Scanning the pile of letters, I searched expectantly for foreign stamps. Our prize, a letter from Lia's Korean social worker, finally arrived. The carefully constructed Korean characters impressed both Neal and me. An English translation followed:

"Jin Jung's foster mother is grateful to you for the presents and make efforts (sic) to take good care of her. Jin Jung will be more prettier and healthier (sic) baby when she comes to you."

Memos from our social worker also encouraged us:

"No one can say your daughter doesn't have an expressive face! Your gifts seemed well chosen. Hope we *might* hear about visa petition approval by end of Jan."

It was still dark as we rushed to get ready. Leaving for the airport at 6:00 a.m. challenged us. Finally, diaper bag in hand, we hurried out into the chilly February morning. A nerve wracking marathon in San Francisco commute traffic contributed to our tension. Ms. Cray, waiting at the Pan Am gate, was joined by a couple of other adoptive families and the Holt greeters. Excitement permeated the air as we eagerly traded stories and pictures of our new children. At last the brand new 747 taxied to the gate. Sunlight gleamed off the cockpit window. As families disembarked we studied every Asian baby. Could this one be ours?

"Look Neal, there she is! Derek and Douglas over here!" All at once we saw our baby cradled in the arms of her escort. "What torture!" I moaned. "I can't stand just seeing her through the window." Suddenly they disappeared down the stairs. As our arms itched to hold her, "customs" came first.

The wait was interminable. Patiently busy with pencils and books, Derek and Douglas showed restraint. "This is terrible! Neal, what are they doing in there? They said it'll be another half an hour." Eventually, a uniformed official peeked out of the swinging doors. "The mothers. Only the mothers," he bellowed.

Maneuvering through the massive crowd of strangers, we instantly bolted for the heavily guarded inner sanctum. Ginny, the greeter, passed six-month-old Lia to me without a problem. Immediately, she melted into my arms. Her head snuggled into my left shoulder. My delicious pink bundle felt sweaty and warm.

Meticulously dressed for the Korean winter, heat rash peeked out from her wrists and booties. Her fine dark baby hair, still untamed, gave her a bit of a wild look. Documents were stamped and we were dismissed, free at last, to take our baby home.

"Lia's fine except when I hold her away from me to try to look at her." Her loud wails emphasized the point. My shoulder became her security.

Even later, as a toddler, she clung to my shoulder. "Mom, that lady's looking at me. Mom." But now I was joyfully astonished! It had been a long time since I had held a baby of my own. We all enjoyed a calm drive home. A dry diaper, cooler clothes and a bottle of milk satisfied Lia.

"Hey guys, come and look at this," I called in a stage whisper. Little Lia, sleeping peacefully, occupied only a tiny spot on our king sized bed. Next to her stretched Neal's lithe 6'3" frame. Dad and daughter were definitely "bonding." From the very beginning, Neal was putty in Lia's tiny hands. Having missed the boys' babyhood, he cheerfully participated in her care. He often did the middle of the night duty and changed many diapers. Later they enjoyed many bike rides together, Lia happily waving good-bye from her kid's seat. Even the surprise of her warm spit up over the back of his shirt, didn't deter their outings. Lia's homecoming was a joyous occasion!

Derek and Douglas showed great enthusiasm for their baby sister. "Mom can we bring the car pool in to see Lia? Come on in guys. This is our new sister! Have a popsicle." She was thoroughly introduced.

It amazed us how this little girl from across the world, who looked nothing like the rest of us, immediately became our own daughter. Our feelings were just as deep and loving as for the boys born to us. There wasn't any difference.

Lia added a lot to our family and I always looked forward to our social worker's visits as an excuse to show her off.

"She's settled into our family so easily. Her 'Bomo' in Korea must have taken great care of her," I exuded. "She readily responds to our attention and affection. That nurturing served her well. We're grateful that she was in a foster home instead of the orphanage."

Both Neal's parents and mine joyfully welcomed her into the family. I was delighted to have *one* baby. It was so easy compared to the hectic pace with twins.

13

Our family adoption group was a real encouragement to all of us. Derek and Douglas met other ethnically mixed families like ours. It helped us feel more normal and less like a "curiosity." Everyone was so proud of their children, which made our get togethers positive and supportive. We compared notes on everything from baby's first steps to the stares of strangers.

We were especially impressed with the orthopedically handicapped kids in the group. Their spunk and stamina seemed unbeatable! Dashing around the picnics, their crutches flew, like regular kids having fun.

Perusing Holt's "Blue Book" of hard to place children compelled me. "Neal, look at these pictures." Scrawny, sad children met our eyes and our hearts. "These kids don't look difficult. They're just pre-schoolers. They're so little. Don't you think we could handle one of these kids?"

These faces touched Neal too. So "stepping out" again, we asked for an older girl with an orthopedic handicap. Besides, we wanted to fill in what we thought was a large five year age gap between Lia and the boys. Older kids needed homes, and seeing the need, we responded.

We expected a little girl who'd had polio just like the kids we knew and admired. But we later learned that it is not a cliche... *God gives you only what you can handle.*

As we watched the DeBolt family expand, ours expanded too. Many of their children had extensive special needs. But what we saw was the joyful way they welcomed each child into their already large family. Could we risk just a little bit more?

"Jeannie, you can do it! We're thinking of getting a little girl to be a sister for Wendy. Karen is just about her age," said Dorothy.

Our conversations uplifted me. Always willing to help other families, their outlook was contagious. Their belief that there is "no such thing as an unadoptable child" challenged us. (The DeBolts later founded "AASK," Adopt A Special Kid. A national adoption agency, it has facilitated the placement of children with special needs into loving permanent families across the nation.)

Soon our plans took a major detour! "Neal, Holt says it'll be two years before the state can update our home study. Can you imagine?" Two years was two years too long!

Now Dorothy came through again:

Dear Jeanne and Neal,

After talking with Elsie today I was very upset at the position you now find yourselves in. Your contacts certainly have not been conducive to enthusiastic pursuit of your goals. However, please, you two beautiful people, DON'T LET *ANYTHING* STOP OR GET YOU DOWN IN YOUR ATTEMPTS TO ADOPT A "SPECIAL CHILD!" There are always certain social workers and/or secretarial staff....who are not particularly sensitive to people's needs. They become too immersed in the mechanics of things.... *However,* there are those other truly dedicated people in adoptions who WILL go out of their way to help you, and who are appalled when they learn of the callous inefficiency of the type worker described above..... At any rate, your present request for a handicapped child is not about to be ignored. Some child somewhere needs and deserves all you have to give. Let's find her!!! Hang in there.

Fondly,
Dorothy

Also our pediatrician had just given me adoption information regarding Mexican children, but we had never thought of it for us. Two families from our area working with a reputable attorney pioneered the process in Guadalajara.

In the midst of this time of mixed emotions, despite the encouragement and my optimism, a wave of sadness swept over me as I listened to Dad one morning. "Jeannie, Mother passed away this morning. She was in terrible pain during the night, so I took her to the emergency room. It turned out that she was hemorrhaging. She died at the hospital."

Many health problems had plagued my mother. Difficult cataract surgery, complicated by detached retinas, left her legally blind. Cirrhosis robbed her of her health and of the striking beauty that graced her younger years. Her fear of cancer and the heartache of her sisters' deaths were emotional burdens too heavy for her to bear. An alcohol related accident cost her the job she loved. If only she had received the help and understanding that she needed. Instead, her doctors provided a quick fix, prescriptions. Her later days were lived in a haze of alcohol, prescription drugs and depression, so I wasn't surprised when her frail body had worn out. Still, the unexpected timing left me reeling in shock.

Her life had begun with such promise! Born in Oklahoma in 1909, she was the fifth child in a hearty pioneer family. When she was barely two months of age, they traveled the length of the continent to take advantage of the free land available to homesteaders. Settling in Alberta, Canada, they staked out their property. When her German father, Samuel, became the first postmaster, the new community proudly took the name of his new baby daughter, "Hilda." My mother is still fondly remembered in Alberta as "Hilda's" namesake. But with a harsh father and many adversities, her life took increasingly sad and painful turns from those optimistic beginnings.

Now it was my turn to mourn. "Neal, I feel robbed. No grandmother for our kids. Your Mom is so far away in San Diego. Lia's still only a baby."

He acknowledged my whining with a warm and sustained hug. I could always count on his encouragement and understanding.

"It's weird, too. With her drinking, I don't feel like I ever knew her as a person. Not the way our kids know us." I had separated myself emotionally in order to survive.

There had been too many hurts. One of the hardest occurred after our honeymoon. Arriving home, we excitedly anticipated tearing into all the beautiful gifts piled up in my parents' living room. Surely, my folks would share our enthusiasm.

Instead of cheerful greetings, we opened the door to a dark stillness. An oppressive nausea overcame me and one look into the back bedroom confirmed my fears. Two comatose heaps lay side-by-side in twin beds. The stench of stale cigarette smoke hung thickly in the air and a pile of cold stubs overflowed next to the bed. Attempting to stifle my hysteria, Neal led me to the car.

"How could they be so thoughtless? They knew we were coming! It's our wedding for heaven sake." Good memories of the warm and fun personality she displayed during my young years have slowly returned. Still, I mourn the relationship we might have had. Many of my feelings are captured by Hope Edelman in *Motherless Daughters*:

> "The loss of a mother is one of the most profound events that will occur in a woman's life, and like a loud sound in an empty house, it echoes on and on."
>
> "From feeling vulnerable to future losses, to fearing they'll die at the same age as their mothers, to sto-

ically enduring motherless weddings, births, holi-
days and celebrations, these women often view life
as a grief-filled obstacle course."[3]

Although I lost my mother emotionally many years before she died physically, I always maintained hope that she
would stop drinking. Now the chances were gone. It was over.
My soft-hearted, sensitive mother was dead. Only my occa-
sional nightmarish dreams reached beyond the grave.
Alcoholism left an invisible but painful scar on my youth.

∽✿ 14 ✿∽

In 1974, dinner with Patsy and Jim was like a reunion. Our good friends and neighbors from Dental school were always fun to be with. We had so many good memories and now we even shared adoption plights. Our conversation was peppered with frustration. "We're number one on the list for a baby from Marin County. Young mothers are beginning to keep their babies. No babies will be available soon....or maybe ever." Defeat was written on their faces. And we had a two year wait with our agency.

Could Mexican adoption be for us? "We can go together. Our priest speaks Spanish. I know he'll help us with the phone calls." Jim burst forth with ebullience. As we made plans, our excitement grew. Secure in our numbers and with a sense of bravado, we decided to look into it.

Everything fell into place so easily it overwhelmed us. The Department of Immigration updated our homestudy; we had our documents translated into Spanish, the priest spoke with our attorney and Neal's folks were willing to stay with our three children. We were dumfounded! But only babies were available for adoption, so we adjusted our thoughts from an "older" child to newborn infant. Motivated to give a needy child a loving home, what did age matter?

Anxiously, we waited for our attorney's call. "You'll hear from Pedro when the baby girls are ready. Then you can fly down, go through the court and immigration procedures, and bring them home," instructed the interpreter. "It should all take about ten days." Thoroughly covered in prayer, doors opened. We were confident that God prepared every step of our path.

"Neal, I can't wait by this phone much longer." My nerves were frazzled. After waiting months for the signal for an immediate flight to Mexico, we were incredulous when the day arrived.

Filled with optimism, we eagerly joined Patsy and Jim at gate 27, San Francisco International. Airports were becoming a familiar part of our lives.

"I can't believe we're doing this!" Patsy's vitality balanced our apprehension.

"It was hard to leave the kids. Lia just says, 'Mommy, bye-bye Mexico.' She obviously doesn't understand what we're doing. But I know this will be a great trip,"

From our first glimpse, Guadalajara enchanted us. With our luggage lost in L.A., we traveled light. "Well, we don't have to worry about what to wear to dinner," we laughed. Not even the monsoon-like rains could get us down! A passing bus soaked Neal as we shrieked hysterically. Should this have been a "clue?" Our trip continued to be an adventure!

Hotel Roma was located in the center of the city's "action." The impressive city plaza stretched out behind us with camera opportunities abounding. Neal's forbearance impressed us. Waiting for just the right moment, he captured the Cathedral's silhouette in a blazing sunset from our rooftop garden. Ever present Chiclet-selling kids darted across the concrete, seeing every passerby as a potential customer. Exotic aromas from sidewalk stands permeated the air. And fancily carved watermelon and mangos on sticks gave the vendor's carts a festive look.

While carefully scrutinizing each handsome Mexican family, we pondered our future. Would we be parents of babies from this colorful country?

Clinging to Neal in the back seat of the rusty and battered taxi, I endured the race through local traffic. Geysers of water sprayed in all directions as we snaked our way through the outlying residential section of the city. Grateful to emerge alive, we suddenly faced a sinister looking garage front office. A dark, handsome, *young* man with flashing black eyes greeted us. Pedro! His warm welcome was promising, but our apprehension grew as the metal door slammed behind us. His more menacing looking partner examined us from the corner.

Pedro spoke no English. He said that *we* were to bring an interpreter. We thought <u>he</u> had one. So smiles, nods and my three years of high school Spanish had to suffice. It worked until we discussed fees. Wisely, he decided to bring a real interpreter to us. Extremely relieved to leave the garage, we headed back to our security, the "Roma." We were concerned that Pedro, still in law school, was already practicing law. Although this was legal in Mexico, it was peculiar and new to us.

At the second meeting Pedro proudly announced, "Two baby girls have been set aside for you in the hospital. I'll go there tomorrow morning to follow necessary procedures. You will be able to get the babies in a few days. My cousin is a doctor on staff so he'll take good care of them."

To help pass the time, we set off to see the sights. But we also had business to do at the American Consulate. It would be an important and challenging hurdle. Conspicuous gringos, we squeezed a small path through the maze of people seated and standing. As we tried to figure out the system, we wondered if our interview would be as difficult as we expected? After meeting every conceivable person in the place, we finally had our "audience" with Mr. Dressier. Of course we'd have to come back *again* to see the man in charge, Mr. Chavez.

Although we were lucky with immigration procedures, Pedro hadn't fared as well at the hospital. "I waited all day to see the director. But at five o'clock they told me to come back tomorrow morning. I'll let you know what happens then."

Mañana, mañana!! Day after day we waited! Straw baby baskets from the local market and hand embroidered blankets stood ready in the corner of our rooms. And each morning, I approached our hotel maids, "Agua purificada para las niñas por favor." We always expected this would be *the day*! What crazy Americans! Beds, clothes, water but no babies.

Three of us crammed into the back of a VW left no breathing room. Neal rode "shot gun" with 70-year-old Dwight at the wheel. Retired and living in Guadalajara, our neighbor's brother was a gracious guide. Hot air blasting through the open windows made our back seat position insufferable. Perspiration poured over me. Dwight narrated the tour, as he fearlessly careened through the city streets.

Dwight proposed lunch at Motel de las Americas. "Neal, I'm going outside. It's too warm and stuffy in here for me." Suddenly feeling nauseated and dizzy, I wended my way through the crowded tables. As I approached the car, my legs buckled beneath me. Lying on the hot asphalt, I was aware but helpless. Large ants crawled around my head. "Oh well. I'll just lie here. I hope somebody finds me soon."

Fortunately, Jim saw me fall. I felt foolish as Neal and Jim dragged me to the chaise by the pool, but the cool, soothing cloth draped across my brow immediately revived me. By the time lunch was finished, Neal felt sick too. Back at the hotel, we all hit the beds!

❦ 15 ❧

At the festive "El Mercado Libertad," provocative odors and a colorful array of fruits and vegetables invited us to browse. Then we met Absolom. His crisp navy blazer identified him as a Mexican official in tourism. Eagerly, he approached Neal and Jim.

"Can you tell me about the new popular philosophy in the U.S.?" His halting English was barely discernable.

Their answer surprised him. Did he expect to hear about Jesus Christ and the grace that He offers!?

"No, no, no. I mean something else. What about Transcendental Meditation?" His many questions occupied the guys, giving Patsy and me plenty of time to shop.

Later that week at "Denny's," there he was again, *Absolom!*

"I've been thinking a lot about what you had to say!" he shouted across the lively restaurant.

Had God brought us all 3,000 miles to talk with Absolom about Jesus!? Each day blended with the next. We had seen enough sights and I really missed the kids at home. My depression loomed like the gray clouds out our window.

"Neal, I wish we could go home. I know we're committed, but will this wait ever end?"

The next morning, the stench of burning rubber jarred my sleep. A streak of sunshine peaked through the crack in the room darkening drapes. I was relieved to see morning. "Neal, what's that smell? Its coming from the vent. Get up!" I yelled while pulling on my slacks. "The bathroom's smokey and its even worse in the hall. Hurry!"

Throwing on our clothes, we rushed to the stairs. Patsy and Jim, in line ahead of us, clutched their treasures....his new leather jacket and her handwoven shawl from Ajijic. As we stumbled to the safety of the lobby, we joined the crowd already assembled. A smoldering fire on the third floor came from the air-conditioning system. Grateful to emerge unscathed, we all agreed, "its never dull here!" I felt sure God didn't intend for us to die in a fire at the Hotel Roma!

Two and a half weeks, and many prayers later, Pedro announced, "It's all set. You'll get the babies tomorrow at noon. Por seguro!"

We were beside ourselves! The names had already been chosen, Teresa Marie Purvis and Susan Elena Satre. Even colorful Mexican baby announcements were waiting to be mailed. Neal and Jim worried about their offices and Patsy and I missed the kids.

With desperation setting in, the timing was perfect. But our hope dwindled with each passing hour. Noon slowly inched to evening. Dressed up and ready to go, we sat at attention all day. At 6:30 *p.m.* the phone rang at last.

"No chance for today but possibly tomorrow. There's a change in hospital directors. This is a problem for us." More days?? How could this be happening? It was our dreariest Monday ever!

Neal and Jim had to leave. We'd been in Mexico three weeks! The children and their patients needed them. None of us could afford such a long "vacation." Our farewell dinner at "Chalet Suizo" was festive, and Patsy and I got a final "pep talk!"

"Everything will be under control at home. You won't have to worry about a thing. Just concentrate on getting our babies. Stay as long as it takes." They were convincing and we were convinced!

In reality, I envied Neal and felt depressed that I had to stay. But we knew the "sacrifice" would be worth it. Patsy and I felt a sense of freedom as we watched them go. The previous tension filled weeks had drained our emotions. Now we hoped to relax. Patsy moved into my room. We washed our hair and walked to the Hilton for lunch. Stopping for magazines and cookies at the panderia made it a fun day. The phone was still our appendage, but we maintained a new spirit of optimism.

16

Before long, desperate calls from home began, "My Mom's sick and Lia stuck her finger through the knot hole in the fence. Chugga, the neighbor's bassett hound, bit her." Neal sounded discouraged.

Jim called too. "Take as long as you need," suddenly became "come home right now!"

Pedro wasn't giving up, so we transferred all of our baby paraphernalia to the home of our California friends. Both "Susans" were now Mexican residents. Seeing their animated little daughters, Ana and Pedra, inspired us. This would be our last visit.

"They must think we're really nuts," we giggled as we lugged baby beds, clothes and bottles of water through the hotel lobby. The waiting taxi soon overflowed with our supplies.

Preparing to go home was a wonderful relief. "I'll pick the babies up at the hospital with Pedro. Since your paperwork is complete, you can fly down to get them," Susan reassured.

Our going away dinner at "the Susans" ran fashionably late. Getting a taxi back to the hotel from their neighborhood became difficult. "It'll probably be easier if you walk to the taxi shelter," instructed Susan.

That sounded workable. But buckets of rain poured over us as we sloshed through ankle deep puddles. It was *dark*, *late* and *threatening*. Hurrying past the park, sinister looking young men hurled unintelligible comments our way. Struck with apprehension, we sped up, water spraying under each determined step. We found no taxis at the shelter, so we returned to Susan's house.

Relieved to be back in the security of the house, we phoned for a taxi and waited. "What's taking so long? I can't believe it's so hard to get a taxi."

Finally one cruised by the house but was instantly gone! "Augh-h-h! They didn't even stop!" Frustration changed to panic as we considered our 8:00 a.m. flight to San Francisco. By now most taxis had stopped running for the night.

"What will we do?" I moaned.

"I'll call the hotel," said Susan. "I wish I had thought of it sooner. Hotel Roma? We have two of your guests who need a taxi. They're stranded here. Please send one right away. Can you do that?"

"It's here Patsy. Get your stuff. Lets get out of here!" They sent us off with a shower of hugs and promises of babies. Exhausted and relieved, we slumped into the rear seat. But our tremulous exploit had just begun! Well past midnight, the streets of Guadalajara were dark, deserted and ominous. Every back street and alley passed before our eyes. Our route suddenly took on a very menacing and hazardous appearance. Patsy and I reacted like teenagers. Pinching each other, we made every scary face imaginable in the darkness of our back seat.

"I'm scared, are you?" I whispered.

Silently we each pondered our fate. If only the driver could speak to us, but the language barrier didn't encourage chit-chat. Time stood still while we wondered if we would ever reach our destination. Then spying the Hotel Roma in the distance, our internal celebration began. As we pulled up to the hotel, our driver ran around to open the door. Grabbing our arms, he escorted us right through the lobby and delivered us to the manager at the front desk! Sincere gratitude overwhelmed us! I'm surprised we didn't kiss him. Instead, many nods and handshakes communicated our appreciation. The man we worried about became our protector that night.

Back home in California, we found solace mixed with the tension of lingering by the phone and waiting. Calls from Susan updated us on Pedro's progress at the hospital. Then the fateful call came two weeks later. Susan's voice sounded flat, "Pedro can't get the babies. The new hospital director says no more babies to North America! Pedro says he's willing to start work with a hospital in another Mexican state. Let us know what you think."

But there was no question! We all agreed that the door to this adoption was closed. Slammed! We all experienced a terrible let down. Our cheerful baby's room now remained depressingly deserted. Susan Elena would never "come home." We were emotionally exhausted, and our children wondered where their baby sister was? Not seeing the babies in Mexico spared us additional heartache that would have made our loss even more traumatic.

But our despair didn't last long. Almost immediately, Patsy and Jim received a call from Marin County.

"Wait'll you hear this!" Patsy was breathless. "They have a little girl for us! She's fifteen months old, has dark curly hair *and* her foster mother named her Teri." It was the same nickname they'd planned for their Mexican daughter!

Then Holt called us, ready to start our homestudy. So we persevered with our original plan, an older child with an orthopedic handicap. And the waiting began again.

🙢 17 🙠

Months later, Nadine's call was just what we'd prayed for! Rushing to her Shattuck Ave. office, we were glad we had a case worker who admired and respected our family. "A *little girl, four years old. I wonder what she's like,*" I mused as Neal battled the East Bay traffic. "I'm surprised that her disability is only in her arm." An infection, chronic osteomyelitis in her arm, was the extent of our information. But we expected a child who'd had Polio.

Parking was always a problem on Berkeley's Shattuck Avenue. Annoyed and anxious, we fumbled with coins for the meter. Nadine ushered us into the back office where we hurried through the usual greetings.

"Before I show you her picture, I want you to know that I'm concerned about the report. She sounded stern. "From the comments written about her, I'm afraid she might be withdrawn. She may even have a severe learning disability."

We were not deterred. "Can't we see the picture first?" Neal insisted.

Jang Eun Yung (soon to be Melinda Eun) was a pretty little girl with a mournfully sad face. Typically, she was found near a police station in Seoul.

"Eun Yung is a 4-year old girl. Seems to be normally developed physically for age, but has been taking treatment due to osteomyelitis. Looks sound intellectually, but is introvertive by nature and is much shy of adults. Not on good terms even with her bomo and does not like to talk. Is shy of stranger. Should take care of her with much concern to de-

velop a good image upon adults even though not so
serious thus far. Medical attention must be concentrated on. Hope she will be adopted into a nice
family immediately to develop sound personality
growing up under warm care of a family since she is
in her most sensitive age. Adoption is available."

"Now, before you give me an answer, I think you should
go home and sleep on it." Nadine attempted her best counsel.

Sleep on it?! Neal and I instinctively knew that Melinda
Eun, "Mindy," was the child for us! We agreed that there was
no need to weigh our answer. The written words meant nothing. After so much waiting and prayer, we were bursting.
Again, it was a joy to see our child's face for the very first
time, to know her name and age.

With Mindy on my mind, I was riveted by the Pastor's
Sunday morning announcement. "There is a need for vol-
unteers to help with the orphan airlift that is coming out of
Viet Nam. 'Laps'are needed at the San Francisco Presidio."

Rushing home, my fingers fumbled as I dialed the number.

"Sure tonight is fine. I'll meet you in the church parking lot and we can drive in together." Being a weekend, it
allowed Neal the time to control our home front. I felt an
instant bond with my fellow volunteers, all new to me. The
hour to San Francisco was punctuated with conversation of
our perceived expectations.

Rushing frantically through the doors of the cavernous
military training hall, we were issued our assignments. "Carol,
Pat, Lynda and I are working as 'laps,'" I called to Judy who
was making her way to her position as Pharmacist. The building teemed with children and zealous helpers! Two plane
loads of children had already arrived. Loud cries and piquant
odors hung in the air. Army issue mattresses covered the floor.

Hundreds of diapers and blankets, stacked along the walls, were all noble donations from local churches and volunteer groups. Doctors, nurses, adoption workers, immigration officials and ordinary "mom's" like us provided the much needed manpower. An intense feeling of goodwill surrounded me.

The whole world watched and cheered as these children were loaded onto the last flights out of war-ravaged Viet Nam. People, working at a frantic pace in Saigon, helped to get the kids out before the government fell. Heart wrenching wails emanated from mothers and fathers as they shoved their own small sons and daughters into waiting hands. Desperate for freedom, emotional scars of pain and sacrifice were permanently etched on their faces. But most of the children were already orphans, tragic victims of war.

Television captured the drama as it unfolded minute-by-minute. One of the last humanitarian rescues was engineered by Ed Daly, the maverick owner of World Airways. A previous C-5A military transport carrying 243 orphans and sixty adults had crashed on take off from Saigon. When a cargo door blew out the ensuing depressurization caused the plane to fatally plummet. Two hundred passengers, 150 children and fifty adults, died that day. Unfathomable scenes of horror filled our television screens. Although injured, Twe and Lee DeBolt, were among the fortunate survivors.

My first assignment as a "lap" was to care for a delicate baby girl enroute to France for adoption. How eagerly she responded to her bottle and my cuddling. Searching her tiny innocent face, I reflected on her traumatic past and life giving future. What a privilege to be part of her journey "home."

Attracted to this worthy and exciting event, we anxiously returned early the next morning. Now "my second baby" was going "home" to Minnesota. Before I knew it, I crowded in line waiting to board a small yellow school bus. Heading for the airport, only a few blocks after we started, the rickety bus sputtered and lurched to an abrupt standstill on a steep San

Francisco hill! While we speculated about what to do next, a California Highway Patrol car screeched alongside.

"We're taking these kids to the airport," announced the officer. "They're holding the plane!" Three of us and our infant charges squeezed into the back of the patrol car and braced ourselves.

"Cadillac move over! Chrysler move over," boomed Officer Mary's microphone. We watched in amazement as the 5:00 clock Bayshore Freeway traffic parted for us.

Hustling through the automatic doors, the airport public address system boomed, "Who can fly to Minnesota? We need one more adult escort."

Boy, was I tempted! But with three small children at home, I didn't think Neal would understand. Instead, I reluctantly handed my sweet bundle to the waiting arms of a flight attendant.

18

Lia impatiently looked forward to having Mindy to play with. We attempted to be an example of calmness as the days inched along. Even though we'd done it all before, waiting wasn't any easier. The peddle of my Singer portable labored as I frantically turned out dress after dress for Mindy. Hand-me-down baby clothes just wouldn't do for a four year old.

While we prepared for Mindy, she was also being prepared for us! Wonderful letters in Korean characters from Holt's Il San Center were accompanied by an English translation:

> Dear adoptive parents of Eun Yung,
> How have you been lately? Thank you very much for sending Eun Yung a thankful letter and wonderful pictures of you. Mindy is anxiously waiting for the time that she will be going to live with you in your country. She is lately absorbed in looking at your pictures, of which she boasted to her friends. Mindy looks very happy. When some of her friends or bomos call her 'Eun Yung', she used (sic) to say, 'You must call me Mindy.'.... Mindy is a comely and intelligent little girl. I can't help kissing on her cheeks as she acts quite cute.... Please pray that she will soon be able to go and live with you. May God continue to watch over you and keep you safe!
> With love,
> Bomo of Mindy

Arrival day finally came two months later, June 25, 1975. Another early morning departure for us and *another* 747.

Would our children think this was the way to have a baby? Go to the airport and meet the plane!? The sweet aroma of homemade chocolate chip cookies filled the kitchen. I wanted everything about the day to be special. Deep in my preparation for the next day's excitement, the persistent clamor of the telephone only annoyed me.

"Jeannie, this is Carol Bennett." Carol and Wayne lived in Los Angeles. What a great surprise to hear her voice. The Bennetts were friends from church. Years before, scrapbooks spilled open across the couch in anticipation of their visit to our home. Lia, an irresistible visual aide, pranced around in her smocked Polly Flinders and Mary Janes. Trying to temper our enthusiasm, we wanted to realistically encourage them with our favorite topic...inter-country adoption. Now our girls were arriving on the same plane!

Hungry for their news, my urgent tasks suddenly became insignificant. I was anxious to share adoption news.

"Guess where we are? San Francisco! We're going to the airport tomorrow."

"Eight a.m., Pan Am from Korea?" I chuckled.

"How did you know?"

"*Our* daughter is coming from Korea tomorrow too. We'll all be there together!" Carol shared my giddiness.

Photos and stories of our new daughters helped to keep our eyes off our watches as we waited at San Francisco International Airport. Derek and Douglas palled around with their boys, Chris and Mike. But Lia's whines persisted over the airport noises, "Uppie, up-eee, I want *Mindy now-ow!*"

The Bennetts spied Janey first. She was a pretty, chubby two-year-old in the arms of her escort. Once more, through a wall of glass, we experienced the invisible barrier.

"Hey, over here. Here she is! Here's Mindy!" Frantically, I gestured to the family so they could get a glimpse of her.

Even though she appeared petrified and exhausted, her beauty shone through to us. What a vision she was in her little yellow and white checked dress, long white stockings, and her hair done up in ponytails. A large white bandage covering her left arm masked the painful open wounds of infection. Although prepared by photos of us, no recognition showed on her somber face. What could she be thinking of these smiling, frantically waving strangers?

Finally, "The mothers come in."

Curbing my excitement, I cautiously approached Mindy and her escort. "See if you can get her to go to the bathroom. No one has gotten her to go with them," were my first instructions from "the lady with the red purse."

Grateful for the Korean language tape, my knowledge was limited to a few essential vocabulary words. Bae-kop-pa meant hungry, Sa-rang-han-da, love you and jam-ja for sleep. The bathroom words came in especially handy!

Mindy had squeezed the color from her escort's hand. Gently prying her fingers away, I stooped to comfort her with soothing words she couldn't understand. Our trip to the bathroom was successful. But she lost her composure and cried in terror as we entered the crowded hall filled with strange sights and sounds. Before long, we had *two* screaming little girls. Lia began to mimic her terror. People stared in awe as we approached with our two sobbing charges. What had we done to cause such unhappiness?

Soon the humming car engine and soothing radio tunes took over. Tears quickly faded into deep sighs and instant naps. An hour later, as we pulled into the driveway, the sleepy girls revived. Our sturdy redwood house, rimmed by fledgling Monterey Pines sparkled in the sunlight and seemed to offer a sincere welcome. Mindy hesitantly laced her petite fingers through mine and took a long look. Then, with quiet determination, she started up the seven stairs to the front door. "Its okay Woo-ree-jip. This is our house," I encouraged. We watched with captivation as she kicked off her little sandals and straightened them neatly by the straw door mat. "God really has opened the heavens and poured His blessings on us today," I whispered while dabbing my joyful tears.

"Come on, Mindy. You got lotsa new toys!" Lia tugged impatiently on her bewildered sister and they quickly disappeared to play. But minutes later Lia emerged screaming, "Mommy, Mommy, Mindy just drank the water out of the flowers!" This seemed like a logical solution for a thirsty child on a sweltering day!

Mindy cautiously guarded a small red satchel which was her only possession. Tucked inside were small gifts for us and a stunning silk Korean dress just Mindy's size. In one corner, we uncovered a tiny homemade scrapbook fastened with yarn. Black and white pictures of Mindy in Korean costume radiated from the carefully pasted pages. A cheerful group shot of her housemates followed, along with photos that we had sent of our house and family. Diminutive flowers, lovingly cut from greeting cards and wrapping paper, edged the pages. The usual souvenirs, rubber Korean shoes, were all we'd expected. In contrast to the initial report, Mindy must have been a favorite of her "Bomo."

"OK, seat belts!" The six of us squeezed into the aging station wagon ready for our first family outing to the park. Sand flew in all directions as the girls raced to the swings. Mindy settled into the child sized seat and I proceeded to gently push her skyward. Then before I knew it, she slipped through the thick canvas straps and hit the sand with a thud. Lying flat her back, her little body was racked with sobs. I was devastated.

Hoping a change of scene would soothe her hurts, we headed to A&W for an early lunch. Mindy tackled her first hamburger and steaming heap of french fries with gusto. It was a small, symbolic stamp of Americana, we thought. We watched in amazement as she carefully rolled her longest fry in a catsup swathed lettuce leaf. Munching away, complete contentment radiated from her face.

Later, Neal and I peeked into Mindy's room from the corner of the hall. From the bright wallpaper border to the colorful print quilt and matching curtains, her room exuded little girl cheerfulness. The maple fourposter had been mine at her age. Dolls, stuffed animals, games and childrens' books poured forth from the floor to ceiling bookcase. And right in the middle of the floor sat Mindy! We watched her meticulously fold doll clothes and sweep imaginary crumbs into her tiny palms. She sang as she worked, "Yum gum bo-la-dee, Yum-gum bo-la-dee." This was an example of the wonderful way she must have helped at Il San, the children's home.

"Look at Mindy, Mom. Her popsicle's upside down!" The kids got a kick out of her fresh approach to life. At Baskin Robbins she just stared at her ice cream, not knowing what it was. Should she trust us enough to try it? And she was adamant with her *Korean* lessons. We, in turn, attempted to teach *her* English. We have warm memories of Mindy's adjustment to our family and the laughter that punctuated our days. But no formal English lessons were needed. Mindy picked up the language quickly through conversation. We learned the importance of flexibility in combining two cultures. Mindy settled in at her own rate. Our patience helped!

Days later, I relished a whole hour alone when I made my trip to the grocery store. But on the way back, horror overcame me as my car rounded the Civic Drive curve. Bolting down the middle of the hectic four lanes of traffic was Mindy, with Neal frantically following in hot pursuit – a dramatic reminder that we were starting at the beginning with her. She had so much to learn.

19

Mindy was still sleeping on the floor, Korean style, when the Doctor broached the subject of surgery. "The wounds on Mindy's arm are serious. Tests show a chronic staph infection. She could lose her arm, if we don't take care of this now. Surgery is urgent."

There was no time for adjustment to her new life. Medical facts took immediate precedent over her psychological well being. Beside her foreign sleeping style, she also didn't speak or understand English. How would she handle such an imposing medical center environment? Reassuring her of our love and commitment to her became paramount to us. A hospital coloring book and a script of our encouragement became my vehicle.

We will be her parents forever. When we leave her at home with a babysitter and brothers and sisters we'll always come back. We all love her very much. Her arm needs treatment and we need to take her to the doctor often so that he can help to make it better. Is there anything bothering her? There are times when she feels sad and we don't understand what's wrong. We try to help her the best we can.

Gratefully, a Korean friend translated, but we were stunned by Mindy's curious reaction. Wasn't she happy to have someone speaking her language? Instead she seemed to view Taihee as a threat. As she reached out with soothing Korean words, beads of perspiration trickled down Mindy's apprehensive brow. Did she think she might have to go back to Korea? How we wished we could perceive her thoughts. Ultimately, the friendship barrier was broken! Mindy's face sparkled as she spied the plastic bag that Taihee offered and the eyes of the tiny dried fish stared back at her. Mindy relished and devoured each one, heads and all.

Mindy's hospitalization was successful, but leaving her there was excruciating for both of us. The imposing aluminum crib that filled her tiny glass walled room and the "Isolation" sign on her door created an intimidating scene. Trusting that her tears would cease, I turned the corner of the hospital corridor.

"She'll be fine, but I'll call you if she doesn't settle down." Although friendly, the nurse sounded stern and parents weren't allowed to stay. Feeling heartless, I hurried away from her wails.

Early the next morning another nurse greeted me anxiously. "Mrs. Satre, Dr. Battat's father died suddenly and he is unable to do the surgery today. You can take Mindy home and reschedule or his partner will operate."

"Take her home? You've got to be kidding!" We'd already experienced the most difficult part, especially the blood test that preceded hospital admittance. Mindy screeched, kicked and spattered every available glossy white wall. Evidence of her healthy red blood was everywhere. "I'm sure his partner will be fine."

I followed the steel crib as it clattered along the corridor to the operating theater. Mindy, inconsolable and unreachable, blasted through the swinging double doors. "Absolutely No Admittance," glared grimly back at me. Left behind, I felt powerless.

My frustration and anxiety immediately surfaced in an explosion of tears. Attempting to compose myself, I hurried to the boys in the waiting room.

Derek and Douglas, eight, wrapped their skinny arms around my quivering shoulders. "Don't worry Mom. Mindy's in good hands. She has a good doctor doesn't she? And think of all the people who are praying for her."

Impressed by their strength and sensitivity, I knew Mindy *was* in good hands!

She tolerated the surgery well. An IV pierced her right hand and her infected left arm was attached to a pump that provided a continuous antibiotic wash. She smiled when I put her favorite toy watch around her *ankle*. Hospital popsicles and ice cream calmed her. She had finally adjusted to the hospital routine by the time she was ready to go home.

"No-oh," Mindy moaned as I helped her dress. Elastic cuffs were intolerable.

Foolishly, I tried to cover her scars with long sleeved shirts and dresses, impractical in our sweltering East Bay summers! But Mindy was not self-conscious.

She answered kids' questions directly, "I broke my arm and had to have an operation." *I* learned the valuable lesson of acceptance from *her*.

Two more operations followed during the next few years, but each one was easier because she understood more. "Now that the infection is cleaned out we'll need to strengthen her arm." Dr. Battat inspired confidence with his clear and matter of fact explanations. "First we'll use screws and wire to fuse her ulna and radius at her wrist. The final operation will be to remove her 'hardware.'" These were simply "bionic parts" to Mindy, a perfect relationship to TV's "Bionic Man."

"Mindy your arm has healed so well!" Neal and I caught the doctor's enthusiasm and were relieved that her arm would function normally. Her beautiful piano playing would have been impossible without these extensive surgeries.

20

Lia's strong-willed, raucous nature contrasted with Mindy's quiet spirit. Lia hated to stay in her crib. If she wasn't in bed with us, we often found her spread eagle, in the nude, sound asleep on the bathroom floor. We always remembered to click on the light so we wouldn't step on her.

"No," "I don't care," or "that didn't hurt," were her typical retorts. Then at four-and-a-half years she gathered up her confidence and calmly declared, "My *real* mother is probably a beautiful Korean princess."

"She probably is, but tough luck sweetheart, you're stuck with me!" Developing a thick skin, I learned not to take her flip comments personally. A sense of humor often spared me hurt feelings. In spite of their opposite temperaments, the girls got along as well as most sisters and they were good playmates.

Growing up with Derek and Douglas was always lively fun and often challenging. Walnut Creek California's small town atmosphere encouraged their regular exploration. Shopkeepers welcomed them and commented on their bright inquisitiveness and polite manner. So when Doug asked to walk to the stamp store, only the time concerned me.

"Doug it's almost 4 o'clock. People will be coming home from work. I don't like the traffic. It's too late!"

Finally, the boys' badgering wore me down, "Well, go ask Mitch's mom. If she says yes, its OK."

A hurried phone call confirmed that the boys were on their way. Later Doug bounded into the kitchen just in time to slide into his place at dinner. Nothing revealed his recent adventure.

"How was the stamp store?"

"Well, everything was fine until Mitch got hit by the car." Doug was nonchalant. "Oh, he's OK. His mom is taking him to the hospital to get x-rayed to make sure he doesn't have anything broken. Some teenagers hit him in the crosswalk," he continued. "Then they picked him up, put him in their car and drove us both home."

"What?!" I went ballistic. "You got in their car? Haven't I told you never to get in a stranger's car?" Scenes of a local kidnapping flashed through my mind. As I poured my coffee, I vowed to thoroughly trust my intuition in the future.

Besides the stamp store, "Martin's Theatrical Supply" was another favorite haunt. Besides costumes and dance attire, they stocked such essentials as smoke bombs, whoopee cushions and magic tricks. We had just returned from church when a great commotion resounded downstairs. Clomping dress shoes, bodies bashing into stairway walls, and shirts being pulled and stretched heralded their raucous burst into the kitchen. Each spurt of ink across their Sunday shirts was accompanied by loud yelps.

"Mom, he's spraying ink on me."

"Help Mom, make him stop!"

Little Lia cowered behind me as I approached the landing.

"And this is for you Lia," one shouted while black ink streamed down the front of her long white Sunday school dress. "Wha-ah-ah," four-year-old Lia's response was immediate and blood curdling. In shock, I tried to help and comfort her, but before I could rally, it was my turn.

"This is for you, Mom!" Again, ink streaked across the front of my buff colored turtle neck. Mission accomplished, Derek and Douglas, nine years old, doubled up howling. "Ha, ha, ha. Its only disappearing ink!"

Lia continued wailing and, still in shock, I reacted by grabbing Derek's hair.

"But, Mom, its only a joke." The hysteria was broken as Neal demanded, "Jeannie go to your room!"

"Go to my room? I'll go to my room all right!" Eventually my fury subsided and only Neal had spared Derek his hair.

Animals played a prominent role in our family. Pets ranged from our first cat "Squeak," to various dogs, hamsters, rats, birds and a rabbit who sprayed us. For awhile, we even supplied the kid's pre-school classes with guinea pig babies. The twenty-four acre field across the street, was a goldmine for reptiles. Alligator lizards often made their home in my shoe boxes! Then the boys graduated to *snakes*! One day while describing a stupid move of mine to Neal, he said, "Don't feel so bad. Go see Derek. I think he's feeling pretty stupid now himself."

"Why?"

"Remember that big king snake Doug caught yesterday? Derek just bought it from him for $7.00. He covered the terrarium with a piece of screen and it's gone. He should have at least put a brick on it." The snake was never seen again. But for a long time, I anticipated a coiled king snake in the dirty sock pile of the laundry room.

Yard sales were always a favorite of Neal and the boys. Doug and Derek shared Dad's enthusiasm for old tools, square nails and other male treasures. Pulling them away was usually difficult. Now everyone was finally settled in our metallic green station wagon. Only one was missing.

"Wait!" Doug ran breathlessly to the driver's window. "Look! Isn't he great? Can I keep him?" The pretty little garter snake flicked his forked tongue in our direction.

"OK, Doug. See if they can find a box for him, but hurry up." With Doug and his pet in the back, we headed home.

Before long, a strange odor wafted forward, the snake's self protection. While we finished unloading the car, Doug, with fifth grade enthusiasm, leaped up the stairs from his room in the basement. "Mom, Dad, the snake just had a baby!"

Wow! We were all impressed. Minutes later,

"Mom, Dad, the snake just had two more babies!" And, "Mom, Dad, the snake had more babies...six... nine...twelve. Hey, the book says that the snake can have up to twenty five babies!"

Although Doug was thrilled, we weren't. He reassured us that he could easily find homes for these offspring.

A few days later, I was just settling into the car when a Buick sedan blocked my exit. "Doug invited Ross to play this afternoon. I can pick him up at five," Pat said leaning out her car window.

"That would be fine but I have an appointment. Doug didn't tell me. He's welcome to come back another day."

While we talked, Ross and Doug disappeared into the house in a flash. Playtime wasn't on their mind, only snakes! Ross came out displaying his prize.

"You may not keep that Ross!" His mother was adamant. "I don't believe in caging wild animals!"

Although embarrassed, I didn't classify a tiny garter snake as a "wild animal." It sounded like we were caging tigers. Ross and his mother left....without the snake.

"I thought it was a good idea, Mom." Doug sounded defeated.

"Selling snakes to the kids at school is not a good idea! How about letting them go in the field? I think they'd be much happier there."

21

"Jeannie, I think you'd better get a babysitter tomorrow and spend some time with your Dad. He has something to tell you." The urgency in Neal's voice left me feeling perplexed and uneasy. "What do you mean he has something to tell me?" Reaching into the depths of my imagination yielded no clues. Could something *that* important have eluded me?

"Jeannie, he knows the identity of your biological mother."

"How can that be? I thought she died in child birth." The cloud of fatigue that had enveloped me suddenly lifted, and I was energized by the curious revelation!

"I've known for quite awhile. Your mother told me late one night after she'd had a lot to drink. Through a lot of tears, she made me promise not to tell. I wasn't sure it was true so I kept the secret."

That alcoholic scenario was all too familiar to me. I was grateful for the way Neal patiently dealt with my mother on such grim occasions. How could I be angry with his silence?

Now the immediate issue was all encompassing. "*Who was she? Was she alive? Why didn't they tell me?*" tumbled involuntarily from my lips. Did Neal really think I could wait until tomorrow to learn this news?

Finally, worn down by my interrogation, Neal disclosed the truth. "She's one of your aunts." A stunned silence overcame me. I had been close to both of my mother's sisters. Family memories suddenly flooded my consciousness.

It could be Aunt Em, but I knew she would have kept me. However, Aunt Eleanor, blond like me, was single then. Maybe it was her. Neal leaned close and whispered, "Look in the mirror." Then I *knew*! I look just like her. Neal couldn't believe that I had not unraveled the mystery of my past.

Nervously, I arrived at my Father's neatly kept apartment. The paintings he enjoyed collecting gave the small space a gallery appearance. Daddy, bundled in his vibrant blue robe, shuffled to the door to greet me. His welcoming embrace was warm as always, but this hug was tighter and longer than usual. I sensed his deep emotion. "Oh Dad, I know what you have to tell me. You know how you always call me a 'needler?' Well, I 'needled' the information right out of Neal last night."

Struggling to contain his tears, he seemed relieved that the news was "out." He choked on his words as he shared from his heart. "I wanted to tell you sooner, but the time was never right. I knew you'd find the papers in my safe deposit box and I didn't want you to find out that way."

"That's OK Dad." It's strange. I was never that curious. I always sensed Mom's sadness. I thought it was because she couldn't have a baby. I never even suspected *this*!"

"I just want you to know how much Eleanor loved you. She was always interested in the best for you. She was a wonderful and brave woman. I'm glad I can tell you that. By this time we were both teary and my heart went out to this man I loved and admired. "Do you want to know who your *father* is?"

"Well, you can tell me the name. But as far as I'm concerned, *you're* my father and always will be." Quickly, before he could stop himself, he blurted, "Chasen Stuart. He lived in San Francisco when Eleanor told him she was pregnant, so he knew. His only response was 'just don't tell my mother.' But, Jeannie, it was during the war. He may have been sent overseas. I don't think he ever saw you."

I didn't ask questions. I was uncomfortable that my Dad, now ill with cancer, would think I was interested in "'my real father." My love and loyalty to my adopted dad was stronger than my curiosity. Besides, as far as I was concerned, *he* was my only father!

But this was an arduous time for me. Besides reading books on death and dying and reflecting on my newly bestowed identity, I was also preparing for my first trip to Europe! A pile of books littered my bedside table.

Since my mother's death three years earlier, my father lived contentedly single. We all enjoyed his new found sobriety and peace of mind. But by July 4th, the U.S. bicentennial, we were struck by the news that Dad's cancer was out of remission. Typically, he presented a stoic and pragmatic attitude regarding his future, but having been born in Scotland, his heart remained there. So, on this sizzling California 4th of July afternoon, we urged him to visit his homeland. "If you have any extra money Dad, why don't you go to Scotland? We'll go with you!"

"Fine. You go with me and I'll pay." A quick call to Neal's mom in San Diego confirmed our hope that she would stay with our four children.

Our excitement was continuous. Each day Dad called overflowing with enthusiasm about his emerging plans. "I wonder if my cousin Annie still lives in Dumfries?"

The last letter from *my* cousin Frank was fifteen years earlier. I remembered the picture of a fair-haired, gangly youth in a sweater vest. So many years had passed since our student days.

One afternoon Dad called. "Oh Jeannie, I'm so glad you're home. I have news that you just won't believe! I'm coming over *now*."

I anticipated hearing the slam of his car door while wondering what he could be talking about. Before he could reach for the bell, I threw open the door and startled him with my raucous greeting.

"I got a letter today from *Scotland*! It was forwarded from my bank (his employer before retirement) to my apartment. It's from Frank. He and Annie are looking for *us*!"

A book about the Patty Hearst kidnapping had jogged Annie's memory. "A 'safe house' in Concord. I wonder if Jeannie and Jim still live in Concord?"

And now Dad's written reply to Frank's letter was eager and immediate. Their ardent correspondence bridged years of silence and mutual feelings of neglect.

Both families joyfully anticipated our meeting in Edinburgh. But two-and-a-half weeks before our departure date, Dad was hospitalized.

"Dr. Davis says a transfusion will build me up. He thinks I can still go."

"Nevertheless his condition inevitably worsened. My letter to Annie was meant to ease her expectations. We couldn't just show up in Scotland without Dad.

Still he was adamant. "No matter what happens, you and Neal are to carry on. I don't care if I die the day you go. You're going!"

"But Dad, I can't do that. I need to be with *you*. Besides it wouldn't be the same, going without you." I gave him my best argument.

"Jeannie, you have to go! Annie and Frank will be disappointed. They're waiting for you. Don't be selfish." How could I object to my father's dying wish? Lapsing in and out of consciousness, he told me about Scotland. Clear boyhood memories flowed from his parched lips. "You'll find the house where I was born. It's on St. Catherine Street in Kirkcaldy. My school is only a few blocks away." My scribbled notes fervently recorded each precious recollection. "On Friday nights brother Jock and I rode our bikes to the Wraith Estate in search of rabbits for Sunday dinner."

"Dad, I can't believe that you can remember all of this!"

A week later, I pondered my complicated past as I watched his form in the hospital bed. My father slept without interruption. Sitting with him allowed me time to reflect on the life we had shared. Thirty-four years that sometimes seemed harsh and long, but now that I was losing him seemed sweet and fleeting. What a gift his recent eight years of sobriety had been to me! And he had made that time count. He put his banking abilities to use by "doing the books" for AA. Sponsoring other recovering alcoholics, collecting paintings and developing a warm relationship with our family helped give his life meaning. And I even had the important encouragement that perhaps he had accepted Jesus, something his private nature wouldn't allow him to share with me. Now his breaths though measured, were shallow, and I was relieved to see him so serene. Despite his advanced cancer, he appeared comfortable and he passed away peacefully... three years after my mother.

We planned the Memorial Service for Friday morning. Thunder, lightening and a deluge of rain punctuated the steel gray day. It was very uncharacteristic weather for October first in California. "Jim would love this," quipped his friend Dave. "He'd say, only his true friends would come out on a day like this!"

By 2:00 p.m. the same day, we were on our way to the airport. Physical and emotional exhaustion encompassed me. I concentrated on my goal, settling my numb body into a tourist class seat.

Two tired travelers from "America" were lavishly greeted by the Scottish relatives. But when confronted with our bad news, Annie attempted to stifle her tears. The disappointment she felt was painful and deep. How she wished she could see "Jimmy" again.

Scotland was just as Dad remembered! His home, his school, and the Wraith Estate were as he described. The kindness and warmth of our cousins helped ease the loss I felt. Our trip would have thrilled Dad! It was an extraordinary memorial journey. The relationships we built with our new "family" would have brought him heartfelt pleasure. And it was deeply meaningful to us to later learn that Annie was, in fact, our sister in the Lord. What a bonus!

22

Only a year later, when renewing my acquaintance with Aunt Em's husband, my interest peaked. Uncle Bill was the only person from my past who knew my history. "I think I have a photo of Chasen and Eleanor. I'll send it to you." The tiny 2"X2" black and white photo helped to romanticize the ideas I had of my biological roots. Had the couple, frozen in time, just stepped out of a Gatsby party? Chasen tall, blond and lantern jawed, stuck a handsome figure in his classic black tuxedo. At his side, Eleanor looked elegant. A gardenia corsage adorned her black strapless gown. Suddenly, I felt proud of my heritage.

Now I knew my beginnings, and when I looked in the mirror I *saw*! I saw Aunt Eleanor! I stole glances of myself in each reflective surface I passed. In addition to her blond hair, I now could see that our facial features were identical. The resounding similarity of our looks made me shudder! My own understanding of who I was had been abruptly obliterated. The perception of my life had been turned on its ear!

Eleanor was *not* a stranger, but someone I had known and loved. We had spent weeks at a time together. I admired her and wanted to be just like her!

From the time I was a little girl, my dress up games paralleled Aunt Eleanor's real life adventures. She led an exciting life with a career in San Francisco. After she married, I loved visiting the city apartment she shared with her husband Craig. And as I got older, I felt grown up taking the train to Fresno to visit her there. It was special to be the *best* and *only* babysitter for my little cousin Allison. I felt much more like her big sister. "Go play with Allison," resounded throughout my visits.

My relationship with Eleanor, though sometimes stormy, had been genuine. I guess we were a lot alike. "Leave me alone. You can't choose my friends. You have no right. You're not my mother!"

Her critical tone often fueled my adolescent impatience. Dissolving into tears, I slammed the door to my room. Although I was only fifteen, we had shared a lot. Most of it was happy.

Many times, laden with carnations, I journeyed by Greyhound to visit her at U.C. Hospital. We spent many hours alone. Though frail and suffering from metastasized cancer, plans were being made for her homecoming. "I'll go to Craig's parents for awhile. When I get stronger I'll finally get to go home. Could you come for awhile and help with Allison?"

Although momentarily encouraged by our visit, my optimism turned to despair when I learned, "Aunt Eleanor is never going to get well." No further explanation was necessary. Emotional pain instantly grabbed my mind and soul. My dear Aunt Em had also died of cancer when I was only six. Why in my brief fifteen years of life did I have to lose another person I loved?

"The funeral isn't for you. It's better to remember her the way she was. There's no reason to put you through this."

Could they really spare me the agony that they had felt with so many family deaths? Now, years later, I realize I never had the chance to say "good-bye." But my resiliency served me well. Busy teenage activities replaced my thoughts of death and loss.

As I looked back, I realized that there would be no opportunities for reconciliations or reunions. *Why had Eleanor declined the chance to tell me she was my mother? The temptation must have been excruciatingly painful. Would it have been a catharsis for her?* I pictured us falling tearfully into each other's arms. But she chose to maintain the secret.

Had she considered my teenage emotions? Would the news have devastated me? She had her husband and his family to consider. Whatever the reason, her decision seemed right. Now I realize her sacrificial gift of love for me. Affection and understanding for her and her difficult life's dilemma swept over me; for I also realized her gift of life.

Eleanor's days of pregnancy had been filled with secrecy and a sense of shame. Following a daily routine, she hid out in her sister's house by day and risked short neighborhood walks after dark. Fear of discovery consumed her energy. *How, she wondered, could she continue to conceal her quickly expanding body from family and friends?* "This isn't working. I have a chance to go away for the rest of the time. It will be easier for all of us."

Gathering her courage, she left the familiar home and city. She was relieved to discover the relaxing atmosphere of the country sanitarium. She formed friendships with women who shared her grim situation and she was finally able to let down her guard. But she felt compelled to resume the charade as she entered the hospital under a new name, Jean Long.

After my father's death I retrieved the papers from the safe deposit box. Reading my adoption release rekindled a spirit of connection to my roots and my past. "I, Eleanor Koch, am the mother of the girl baby born August 14, 1942 at the University of California Hospital where I am registered as Jean M. Long. This baby is known as the child of my sister Hilda Dorothea Murray and on my departure to Hawaii I leave this baby with my sister to continue to raise her as her own and to be known as her daughter. Whatever may befall me, I give to my sister Hilda Dorothea all claims to Jeanne D. Murray." Seeing Eleanor's familiar signature brought tears to my eyes.

Then my thoughts turned to my cousin Allison. How surprised she would be to learn that we were actually half sisters. I'd always dreamed of a sister. I wondered if she would share my excitement and enthusiasm.

Allison jumped at the chance to have lunch with me. We had so much to catch up on. I was now a "mother" and she was a "college student." Many years had passed since our last visit when I had attempted to teach her how to sew. The small Mexican restaurant she selected was dark and intimate. Little did Allison know that it was the perfect atmosphere for revealing my "news."

"Was Uncle Jim sick very long before he died?" she asked hesitantly.

I got right to the point, "Allison, Uncle Jim told me something I think you would be interested in." I forged ahead without stopping for breath. "Eleanor is *my* mother too!"

A skeptical stunned look swept over Allison's face, she trembled as she leaned closer for the details. I could see that it would take time for her to digest the news.

A series of phone calls followed in the ensuing weeks. There were questions she needed to ask. "Didn't you a... feel funny? I mean doesn't it bother you? How do you feel about...?"

"Allison, you mean about being illegitimate? About Eleanor having a baby before being married?"

Her "Uh-hum," was barely discernable. "Allison, I'm adopted. I always assumed I was probably illegitimate. That doesn't really bother me. As far as Eleanor goes, I knew her as a real person. I loved her and at times fought with her too. It was a true relationship. I can accept her as a person who made mistakes. We all make mistakes!"

It was a privilege to help Allison "know" her mother who died when she was only four-years-old. Her idealized version was balanced by my actual memories. As we shared, our new "sisterly" relationship slowly grew and flourished.

However, another reality of my birth was less pleasant. The family cancer history, that I had glibly dismissed, suddenly was my own. Now it was *my* grandmother, *my* aunt and *my* mother who had died of breast cancer. None of them had lived past forty. This realization left me fearful and confused.

By this time I had been married for fourteen years and was the mother of four children. Our blond, lanky twin boys were nine years old. And our beautiful raven-haired daughters, adopted from Korea, were four and five. Besides feeling that one set of twins in a family is enough, my own adoption motivated me to reach out to another child.

As I sorted out the questions concerning my new identity, my heart went out to both my "mothers." Having both biological and adopted children, I identified with both of them. It was an abysmal thought, having someone else raise my twin boys. No vow of silence could keep me in the background. Mother love welled up inside of me. And at the same time, as an adoptive mother, I wondered how I could raise my daughters if their adoptive mothers watched my every move. Compassion and gratitude overwhelmed me. I realized I was very loved. My "mothers" had set aside their own needs and desires to do what was beneficial for me.

23

"Have you heard anything about Chasen Stuart?" Loretta's query jogged my memory. I hadn't thought about my biological father in months. "You know, Roy said he can run him through the computer files. At least we'll know if he has a California driver's license." It was good to have an ally in law enforcement.

I was only vaguely interested, "It would just be good to know if he's *alive*. With my risky genes, I can use the encouragement. Maybe my paternal genes are better." But no information was found.

Months later, Neal and I ecstatically entered our Alta Mira bungalow perched high above San Francisco Bay. It was always a joy to anticipate revisiting our honeymoon hotel. Respites from the kids were essential for our sanity and nurturing of our relationship. As I flopped onto the bed, Neal hefted our bags. A shiny new San Francisco phone book struck an imposing presence on the bedside table. *"I might as well look one more time,"* I thought to myself. Furtively, I flipped through the massive book. Suddenly, as if in neon, THE NAME flashed before me.

"Neal. Come here! You won't believe it. Look!" I was incredulous. "*Chasen Steuart!* I thought it was *Stuart*. No wonder we couldn't find him."

Neal bounded over to the bed with enthusiasm. "I'm calling him!!"

"Look Neal, I don't want to ruin this man's life. You have to be discreet. Don't stir up his family."

Neal tackled this assignment with fervor. His unwavering determination concerned me. Hearing the clicks of the telephone dial, I hid out on the deck.

"Please Lord. If you don't want us to contact him, let him not be home," I repeated over and over. "Oh no. He's talking!" My palms cradled my flushed cheeks.

"Hello," a feminine voice answered.

"Is Mr.Steuart there?" Neal was steady. Silence permeated our room until, "Mr. Steuart? This is Neal Satre. I'm a friend of your family. My wife is the daughter of Eleanor Cooke. Eleanor died of cancer in 1958. I have reason to believe that you are my wife's father. And I just wanted to know if you'd like to know more about her?"

Moments of stunned silence followed, "I'm sorry. I don't think I can help you." There was no denial or feigning ignorance. Although rejected, my sympathy went out to this unfamiliar man. I envisioned him, old and rumpled, watching the Sunday Giants game, minding his own business. A sense of sorrow invaded me. Was he missing out or was I? Would getting to know our family remain an unopened gift in his life?

But Neal was undaunted, "That's it! Tomorrow we have *got* to go by his house."

I wasn't convinced. "What if he lives in Sea Cliff or some other prestigious neighborhood? How will I feel if he's rich?" Fantasy flooded my imagination.

Early the next morning we perused the city map. The Steuart home was only a couple of miles from the dental school neighborhood where we had lived for three years! Anxiously, Neal drove up the Clarendon hill and branched into the residential area. As we approached his street, I was relieved to see the modest but neatly kept row houses. Nothing threatening.

"Well, there's his house." The aquamarine stucco home had a postage-sized lawn and was lined with colorful annuals. "No one's home. Lets get going! I'm a nervous wreck."

But the exploration wasn't enough for Neal! Arriving home he said, "O.K. Now we have to write to him. Right now he doesn't even know who we are. We have to give him a chance to contact us." His persistence confounded me!

Neal's office letterhead gave our correspondence a professional presentation:

> Dear Mr. and Mrs. Steuart,
> You were friends of our family in the '40's... Em and Bill Radonich, Dot and Jim Murray and Eleanor Cooke. Your name recently came up at a family wedding. We didn't realize you were living in the area. In case you would like to contact us, my wife Jeanne and I live at...address and phone number.
> In Him,
> Neal Satre

Neal enclosed a picture of us with our four children and *my* birth date secretively penned on the back.

Again, no reply. I was prepared and although I didn't expect one, my fantasy revolved around a lunchtime meeting. *"Entering the dark and cozy S.F. restaurant I would immediately recognize him. While struck by his warmth and caring, he would be impressed with the quality of my character. Our meeting, stayed at the surface level. Information about his nationality and profession proved fascinating. Did I have siblings?"* I didn't long for a relationship. Despite my family problems, I'd had a loving father. That one time meeting was never to be.

24

Frequently during the following years, I checked the obituaries in the *San Francisco Chronicle*. I hoped that at least Chasen Steuart was still alive. So several years after our letter, while settling down with the paper late on Friday afternoon, I noticed a name emblazoned over a *column* on that page titled "Deaths."

The unusual spelling caught my eye, "Steuart." And then I read on..."Victor Steuart, an undercover detective, was responsible for breaking the largest counterfeiting ring in the history of California." Among his survivors were listed *Chasen Steuart* and his *nephew* Bradley.

"Oh my goodness, I have a *brother*!" I marveled to my myself.

The ringing phone interrupted my thoughts.

"Oh hi Derek. You won't even believe what's in the paper today."

I enthusiastically related the column and then I got to, "Rosary tonight at Haskins Mortuary and funeral tomorrow."

Derek, a student at the University of California in nearby Berkeley, responded immediately. "Mom, I'm going!"

"Well that's O.K. Derek. But I don't want to ruin these people's lives. Don't do anything that will be upsetting. It's not fair to them."

"O.K. Mom, but I really want to go."

That was fine for Derek but I didn't even consider it for me. I had no desire to hop in the car and buck the rush hour traffic. Years later I wondered *why* my curiosity wasn't peaked. Having a houseful of little children must have limited any thoughts I might of had of running off to honor a stranger.

But later that evening Derek called to report, "Gee Mom I think they thought we worked there. I took Chris with me

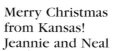
Merry Christmas
from Kansas!
Jeannie and Neal

Chasen and Eleanor
Biological parents

Allison, my
cousin/my
sister and Me

Derek and Douglas

Lia, our first daughter
(Kim Jin Jung)

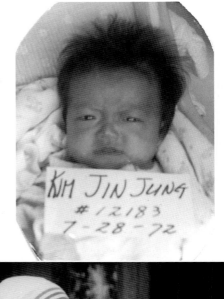

Jang Eun Yung/Mindy
in Korea

Mother Teresa and Kari (1977)

Veena/Kari

Nina/Resa

Mohan/David

Kari and Resa

Lia and Mindy
in their Han-boks

Emmanuel/Stephen

Stephen, what a
cute kid!

Resa still smiling!
2½ weeks in traction

David's Homecoming

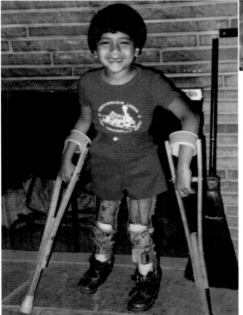

David's first braces
and crutches!

Rebecca and
Joni Eareckson Tada

Niece Julie, adopted
from Korea and
nephew Joseph who
went home to Jesus at
six years old

Elena, our summer visitor
from the Chernoble area

Daughter Lia serving
the Lord in Mexicali,
Mexico

Kari, David and Resa
with Sister from
Missionaries of
Charity–before meet-
ing Mother Teresa in
San Jose, CA (Stephen
was there too!)

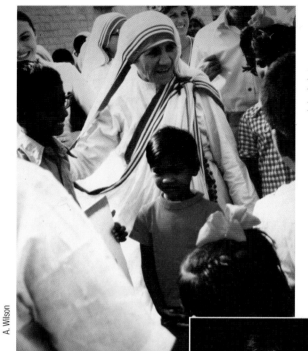

A. Wilson

Mother Teresa visiting the children's home in Delhi

Derek and Douglas' high school graduation

The whole family!

and they came up and said, 'Thank you for everything. We'll see you tomorrow.' It was so weird." Derek at 6'5" would hardly be inconspicuous.

"Well, what were they like?" I strained to hear more.

"They were nice looking older people. The ladies had little perms, they were all nicely dressed and drove new Cadillacs."

"Well, did you see Chasen?"

"Yea, Mom. I saw him. But guess what? He's as bald as a billiard ball!" Derek, who already had a receding hair line, sounded discouraged. But then he perked up, "I'm going back tomorrow."

"O.K. but be careful."

Why did I feel so protective? And then, once more, I got the report! "It was nice Mom. There were a lot of people at the church. I asked the lady next to me if his mother was there. 'Oh no, Martha's ninety and is in the home,' she said."

Ninety? That encouraged me!

"They gave him some Sons of Italy Award. I guess that makes us a little Italian, huh? I signed the guest book, Mom."

And that was that! No news, nothing more. Now ten years later I sometimes wish I'd been more curious. I could have seen my birth father and half brother.

But I loved the scenario. Knowing that Derek went "under cover" to the "undercover" detective's funeral!

But that was the end of the news of Chasen Steuart. He's no longer in the phone book. Has he died? Or, fearing the worst, did he get an unlisted number? I'll probably never know the handsome blond man with the lantern jaw that smiles out to me from a 2X2 black and white photo. And that's okay, because God blessed me with a father who loved me and gave me a life filled with meaning and purpose, much like our heavenly father gives eternal life and purpose to each of His children.

25

We were happy with our perfect little family of two boys and two girls, but something continued to stir us. "You know, Neal, we have a lot of love to give and enough materially." I thought out loud. "Don't you want to share it?" Neal, as always, was attentive to my ideas. "Each of us could get along with half of our possessions," I continued. "And I'll bet we'd be better off."

"There certainly is an amazing need. Kids are really hurting. The DeBolt's example is pretty inspiring," Neal responded earnestly. At the same time, our character could be strengthened. We both agreed on our attitude of outreach.

Our lives had been stretched many times through phone calls. Another adoptive mother, my friend Elsie's words always encouraged me and I benefited from her wisdom and experience. "Jeannie, I wanted to call to tell you about our new daughter Sony. She just arrived from India, our 12th child! India is granting non-preference visas. Sony came from Mother Teresa. If you're interested, I'll give you the information."

Energized by her enthusiasm, Neal prodded me to write and find out about the procedure, but after Mexico, we had no interest in traveling to *any* birth country. Lia and Mindy had already used the two visas per family the U.S. law then allowed (this law has since been changed). Non-preference visas were a new and unexpected opportunity. So I sent my first letter to Kathy Sreedhar, Mother Teresa's liaison, in Washington, D.C.

"Neal, there's no way at thirty-four that I want to have an infant. I'm much too old!" That's a funny statement by today's standards. Our friends, all with two children, didn't identify with our large family.

"How about a 1-3 year old?" Neal concurred.

"Another girl might be best, since Lia and Mindy are the youngest." I liked his idea.

"And we'll consider a child with an orthopedic handicap again. OK?" Neal's enthusiasm was mounting.

The agency showed interest in our family and readily accepted our application. Now, we faced the time element. How could I prepare for our new daughter? The age range made planning impossible and caring for four active children kept my imaginings to a minimum.

With Neal and the boys off to a basketball game, the girls and I snuggled down in front of our favorite Friday night show, "Donny and Marie." Enjoying our relaxation, the din of the telephone was a jarring intrusion. But I couldn't have been more surprised! Friday night was certainly an unusual time for adoption news. My amazement quickly turned to turmoil.

"I know this isn't exactly what you asked for. However, it's an unusual situation and you may just be the family we're looking for!" Kathy sounded sure.

Instinctively I knew my response, and my trembling voice, revealed my distress. "No! Not twins!"

"Well, since you've raised twins," came the telephone retort.

"Nine-and-a-half is hardly raised!"

"Well, they're two-month-old girls in Delhi and one of them has something wrong with her hip. She has to go to therapy every day."

My answer was immediate and tumbled from my tongue without a second thought. "There is no way I can do that Kathy. I have *four* other children to take care of!"

With reluctance, Kathy finally accepted my explanation. But by the time the receiver hit its cradle, my stomach was churning. Rushing Lia and Mindy off to bed, I was left alone with God and my thoughts. There was no hesitation in my feelings. First I called Elsie. Surely she would support me. No answer. Then I freely prayed that God would speak *His will* through Neal. I was certain that he'd feel the same way I did!

As car doors slammed, I lingered in the kitchen waiting to be discovered. Still feeling numb, I was fairly certain that the "twin issue" was settled. Before I could relate the details, Derek and Douglas started dancing around the room.

"That's' great Mom! Just think, we can help two kids instead of one! We'll help you!!" *That* comforted me!? Like when they promised to feed and care for a newly acquired puppy.

Neal withheld his immediate reaction, but I was sure he'd realize that having twins again was impossible. Undoubtedly he'd remember one of the reasons that led us to adoption was no more twins! It was too hard. Besides, these babies were *infants* and had special needs. Who'd want to tackle such a big parenting proposition? I knew *I* didn't!

While searching the Bible for guidance, we discovered some hard hitting words, "Water to a thirsty man is like good news from a distant land" and "Deny the cries of the poor and your cries will be denied." Neal overwhelmed me by enthusiastically blurting out, "My gut reaction is to say *yes!*"

Although nervous, I also felt God's direction and it seemed excitingly clear.

Emotionally spent, I slept undisturbed until shooting up at 7:00 a.m., perfect timing to call Washington D.C. Persuasion was now our task at hand. *Could we convince Kathy that we truly desired to bring the twin baby girls into our family?* It took awhile for her to understand. Could I change my mind that dramatically in a twelve-hour period? Neal's unexpected positive reaction, Derek and Douglas' enthusiasm, plus the confirmation of Scripture made it exhilaratingly evident.

Maybe we weren't looking for twins, but God was looking for us! This was the next step in *our journey of faith*.

Once the decision was made, I accepted the fact I would be "mom" to two more babies. When the pictures arrived, I immediately fell in love with these beautiful girls with dark saucer eyes. From then on my heart was at peace. However, the logistical problems in getting them here and our concern for their health was just beginning.

Non-preference visas meant waiting on a long list. As soon as the girls were assigned to us, non-preference visas were curtailed and many months of bureaucratic frustration stretched out before us. The most emotionally challenging part of each adoption involved the immigration procedures. Each time Neal and I had to be finger-printed. This sounds easy, but appointments were elusive and it was just one of many pieces of necessary "red tape."

After sending the finger-prints to Washington D.C., more waiting ensued. Papers were "lost" and others never reached the proper department. Someone else's prints were even sent to *me*! Ultimately, I was able to get an inside number for a *person* at the Department of Immigration. I'm sure that valuable number was worth money! But more than once, the secretary would say, "He's not at his desk. I'll have him call you back." Click! How could she hang up before asking for my name and number?

Correspondence with India was also particularly arduous. It was an occasion for celebration each time a letter arrived. We hungered for any news of "our babies" and developments in their documentation. Each morning, I anxiously anticipated the arrival of the mail.

26

Our girls, originally "Nina and Veena," were changed to "Paige and Scarlett," and then back again. Subsequently, we by-passed those names. Kathryn Suschiel ("Kari"), and Teresa Jhoti ("Resa"), fulfilled India's requirement for an Indian name.

Thinking that the girls soon would be leaving for the U.S., they were moved to the office of the Director of the children's home. Now their care was personalized, but no one realized what a long delay there would be in their home-coming. If we would have known, I doubt if we could have endured it.

Meanwhile, I anticipated the development and social-ization needs of our infant girls. With such a small staff of sisters, I realized that most of their days would be spent con-fined to their small cribs. Boobie, their main caregiver, was hearing impaired and non-speaking, so I worried about their language development. Many restless nights were affected by my vivid imaginings. A feeling of helplessness and con-cern for our babies gnawed at me. Later I was relieved to learn that Boobie had doted on our girls.

But once again the babies were moved, this time to the home of an Australian family. Joyfully I tore into Janelle's letter. Every detail grabbed my heart. Welcoming Kari and Resa into her family, she adamantly worked to bolster their strength and stamina. Mom Janelle, her Australian newspa-perman husband, and two young blond sons showered the girls with love and attention. Soaking it all up, the babies blossomed!

Each letter, brought me closer to the day-to-day experi-ences of our children. Amused by Janelle's Australian terms, like "changing the girl's nappies," the warmth of her care and devotion shone through the lines.

> "The twins are a delight and quite often I find one of them missing. My husband had taken them into the office. They love bashing on the typewriters and playing with empty cassette boxes." And, "Teresa is the more daring in her eating habits but once she shakes her head and says no that is it. She has a very determined personality as you will discover."

As the weeks and months of waiting multiplied, we also received reports from the director of the Children's Home, Audrey. Not all of the news was positive. Resa had contracted polio as an infant. Both her hips and legs were affected. And then more information followed.

> Dear Jeanne and Neal,
> I feel so sad to tell you the shocking news, little Veena has also had a slight attack of polio. It is so slight that even Janelle who has been with Veena daily, did not notice any difference until she tried to get Veena to crawl. As you can tell from her letter, Janelle is extremely upset. I am enclosing the muscle chart for Veena also. Kathy assures me that you will still want to take them, so I have applied for their passports.
> Yours sincerely,
> Audrey

And:

> "The Satre twins are now down at Commissioner Lane. I have written about Veena's new found problem and so far have not received a reply. I hope it will be alright. I have arranged a therapist to go down

every day and give therapy to them both. This will
cost 50 rupees per month, so please ask the family
to arrange to send this money."

As other correspondence followed, each letter seemed
to detail more problems than the one before.

"Twins: Nina and Veena. The one with polio is quite
badly affected. The leg just hangs sideways, and the
whole side is affected even the eyelid. The other
one continues to do well with Janelle."

Every letter ended, "Do you still want them?" Undaunted, these babies were our own!

Although our commitment was complete, still *not complete* were the immigration procedures. The wait dragged on
interminably. Not taking "no" for an answer, I appealed to
our Congressman. A special Bill would take care of our problem, but his reply was disconcerting,

"I am sorry I am unable to help you with the adoption process of your twin girls from India. I feel that
it would be contrary to my support of adoptions in
the United States."

How illogical! The procedures were all but concluded.
If we were merely inquiring, encouraging us to adopt state-
side might make sense, but doesn't every homeless child
deserve help? Holt's motto "Every child deserves a home of
his own" rang true to us.

My helplessness and the futility of the system prompted
my creativity. Jimmy Carter was President in 1977. A spiritual man, he also had an interesting mother, Miss Lillian. As
a 60ish widow, she had served as a nurse in India. Surely,
she'd have special compassion for our babies. Could she possibly exert motherly influence over Mr. Jimmy Carter,

President of the United States? With ecstatic anticipation I ripped open the hand addressed envelope. The letter, postmarked Plains, Georgia, reached my California mailbox with postage due. I felt assured that "Miss Lillian" would help us, but, all at once, my joy turned to disappointment.

> Plains, GA
> Aug. 28th
> Dear Mr. and Mrs. Satre,
> I am sorry I have *no* influence with persons who handle visas... I wish you much luck... I cannot even tell you to whom you should appeal.
> Sincerely,
> Lillian Carter

The cogs in the bureaucratic wheel slowly inched along while my empty arms ached.

Pregnancy *and* adoption bear their own unique concerns. When physically pregnant, need for proper diet, rest and exercise consumes you. Adoption questions loom up just as strongly. Are they getting cuddled and cared for? Do they have adequate nutrition? Are they being stimulated or do they lie in their crib all day? Are they clean? Have they had inoculations? When will the visa come through? Will they have an escort available for the flight? Our conclusion-there is *no* easy way to have a baby!!

Each shred of news was important. But our biggest thrill was the black and white photos from Janelle... not only of Kari and Resa....but with *Mother Teresa* holding them! "Veena's" tearful scowling face showed that she was unaware of the impressive and Godly woman who held her. The picture became even more precious after Mother Teresa was awarded the Nobel Peace Prize. The enlarged, framed photo continues to hang on our wall *and* the wall of the Children's Home in Delhi.

27

Morosely, we observed Kari and Resa's first birthday without them... *ten months* after they were placed with us "on paper." Our next goal was to have them home for Christmas, but we suffered another failure. At last, our Congressman relented and decided to help us with special visas for humanitarian and medical reasons.

All of a sudden, in a state of panic, I chose traveling clothes to send to Delhi. They were dresses and delicate hooded sweaters, pink for Resa and blue for Kari. The baby room was dusted off and ready!

With only one day's notice, the six of us scrambled to prepare for another early morning drive to the San Francisco Airport. Excitement, anxiety and apprehension churned and ebbed within me. Considering the reports we'd received, we wondered about the girls' condition, but we *were* sure that they were ours!

Two dark, curly headed baby girls peeked over the huge red airline blankets that enveloped them. Escort Debbie was gorgeous, dressed in silk. Each of her five Indian charges, a ten-year-old girl, two young brothers and our babies, looked their best. "Well, I wanted them all to look good for their families. You should have seen us an hour ago. I had my jeans on and the kids were a mess."

From the beginning, Kari and Resa bubbled over with affection and personality. Easily reaching out to us, their transition was immediate. Kari, just beginning to toddle, was fascinated with the irregular rocks on the wall of the airport lobby. Derek and Douglas entertained her energetically while sleepy Resa snuggled in my arms and slurped contentedly on her bottle. A partially healed infection under her eye was the distinctive badge needed to identify our twins. With each adoption, I worried about being "cloistered!" Would I ever see the light of day? I anticipated missing my small amount of "freedom." Instead, I enjoyed being at home with our new arrivals.

Kari and Resa were a joy and everyone loved being with them. But a problem did arise. Small pimply bumps on their beautiful dark skin were diagnosed as "Molluscom Contagiosum." Even the name sounded vile, but this very contagious skin problem is commonly found in places such as Children's Homes. So they were "homebound" and we were gowned and gloved to guard against infection. How Kari and Resa sweltered in long sleeves on warm spring days! Time went on but the persistent infection continued. One area would clear up but more would appear. Resa's physical therapy was postponed indefinitely. *Could she infect other children already in delicate health?* We were finally referred to a dermatologist who performed a biopsy on one bump.

Muluscom Contagiosum? No. Sand fleas, a common Bay Area problem! These tiny vicious creatures feasted on our baby girls.

So our life eventually returned to "normal", whatever that was! Our first family outing with the babies was to the Sun Valley shopping mall and just our *number* made me feel conspicuous! There was Neal and me, our tall gangly blond boys, our middle sized Asian girls and two dark curly-headed babies in the double stroller. *What could people be thinking, I wondered?*

Suddenly, a lady rushed up and grabbed me by the arm, "May I ask you a question?"

"Oh, boy," I thought, "here it comes!"

"Where did you get your sweater?"

That ridiculous question taught me never to be concerned by peoples' frequent stares and curious glances. I gave up wanting to know their thoughts!

Many grandmothers approached with, "Honey, you are so wonderful to take in 'those children.'"

"You'll have a special place in heaven for what you're doing." Although I assumed they meant well, none of those comments felt good to me.

Conversely, I expected every East Indian person to reach out to our girls in unconditional admiration. Surely each of our children was irresistible to those of their own nationality. Although unrealistic, my attitude served our family well. With pride in our children, we were confident of our relationship with them and their homeland. Our enthusiasm seemed contagious.

The grocery line stood still and, with time to scrutinize the two sari-clad women in front of me, I considered my approach. Then I stammered the obvious, "Are you from India?" Their affirmative answer left me flustered. "We have twin girls adopted from India. They're just turning two."

"You do! How interesting!"

Struck by their warmth and friendliness, I spontaneously invited them to meet the babies. A few nights later, we excitedly set out the sweets and coffee for our special guests. All the kids loved company and Kari and Resa raced to the door with exuberant giggles. The mother and her articulate college age daughter, Geeta, arrived with gifts straight from India. It was a friendly and informative evening and, of course, Kari and Resa loved the attention! A few weeks later, two familiar faces (our Indian guests) peered out from the *Contra Costa Times*. "Neal, look! Here they are!"

"Godmother to a Nation" read the headline.

"Madhuben Shah is one of the godmothers of the gentle giant known as India, a massive youngster of a nation. 'Just doing what I'm supposed to,'she says of her voluntary post with the democratic regime of Prime Minister Moraji R. Desai. Shah helps dispense an enormous trust fund whose interest alone pays for the education of poor but brilliant young citizens....She will be the guest speaker for the monthly meeting of the American Association of University Women.

Shah was born into poverty but determined at an early age not to make it a life sentence. Her husband was also born with miserable prospects for economic security, yet together they managed to pull themselves up through the caste ranks. Today, her husband is a successful lawyer and Shah is busy returning to the system some of the fruits it rationed out to her little family. She is modest about the importance of her job, yet the impact of her work could be the impetus that would eventually lift India from the dregs of poverty…"[4]

"I guess I'm a pretty good judge of character," I boasted.

28

Resa finally started therapy for her post-polio condition and tight hip muscles. For several years, on Tuesdays and Thursdays, I bundled her into her car seat to go see "Fernie." It was a fun time with exercises for Resa and instruction for me. The stretching of her contracted muscles continued at home. Only time, in my already busy schedule, posed a challenge. But Resa and I always had special sessions together.

During those early years, Resa wore several braces. The one she hated the most encircled her waist and kept her from bending over. It was cumbersome and hot, especially during the summer months.

"Look Jeannie, Resa's standing," Neal was exuberant. Kari could already walk so her progress thrilled us. Standing on one foot, the weak polio leg quivered along side, but that didn't stop her. Her determination and our encouragement finally led to her first steps. Keeping up with Kari kept Resa on the go.

Then the important day finally arrived. "She looks so cute. I feel like we're deceiving her." But three-and-a-half year old Resa confidently skipped into Mt. Diablo Hospital. She insisted on wearing her party dress and Mary Janes and her favorite purse held her little treasures.

Neal agreed, "Jeannie, Resa's never going to trust us again! She thinks this is a special occasion." Hadn't she understood our explanation?

Again, we had Dr. Battat to assure us. "The surgery released contractures (tight tendons) in both hips. It went very well."

Resa, still groggy, was wheeled in from recovery. "She looks so tiny. Can she tolerate those casts for 2 1/2 weeks?" I whined. Outwardly calm, my stomach churned.

"Man, she is really strung up!" Neal mused. Totally im-mobilized, casts covered both of her tiny legs, one up, one down, both in traction. Only post operative nausea tempo-rarily stifled her giggles. Resa's incredible, sweet spirit and cheerful nature endeared her to everyone. She became the "mascot" of the nursing staff.

Cartoon jingles emanating from pediatrics greeted me. While rushing through the corridor, I suddenly glimpsed Resa's brilliant smile shining through the metal crib slats.

"Resa! What are you doing out here?" I shrieked. "Why are you in the middle of the nurses' station?"

Resa joined in our laughter at my surprise. "Oh, she was lonely and we wanted her out here with us," exclaimed her nurse.

Resa beamed!

Of course *we* were the "entertainment." Story tapes, playdough, magnetic boards, magic slates, coloring books and even bubbles! Anything she could do lying flat on her back. Everyone's attention kept her happy! Resa continued to do well. With her hips fixed, she wore only a small plastic brace on her lower left leg. It fit in her shoe and she put it on her-self. She joined the other little girls in ballet and gymnastics classes and later even mastered riding a two wheel bike. She thought she could do anything! Resa and Kari always sparkled with enthusiasm, and their positive dispositions often inspired others.

When I arrived at pre-school, Mrs. Foster greeted me. "You should have seen the girls today. They sure like each other, don't they? The other mothers couldn't believe it." I waited to hear the rest. "They were playing in separate rooms and when they came to the story circle and saw each other they collapsed in hugs and giggles, 'Kari, where have you been? I missed you!' Those girls are something else! The mothers want to know what you do to teach them to like each other so much?"

But all incidents weren't quite so affirming. After dinner Kari came flying into the kitchen in her stocking feet. Sliding into the bench, she bashed her forehead on the hard edge. The antique school bench that had once held eager students now had marred my daughter's face.

"Daddy, we need you in the kitchen," I bellowed over Kari's piercing wails. Blood poured forth from her face.

"Now Kari, you'll be fine. Get some ice, it'll help the swelling." Neal, as always, remained calm.

"Neal, Kari needs stitches."

"No, I think a butterfly band-aid will be fine."

"Neal, she's a girl! It's not like Doug when he cut his head. She's a girl. It's on her eye."

"No, the band-aid will work."

"S-T-I-T-C-H-E-S!!" I insisted.

"Jeannie, this is fine." Neal was firm.

Hadn't he heard me? "S-T-I-T-C-H-E-S!!"

"Let it be. She's fine. The butterfly is perfect."

Giving up my stand, I cuddled Kari. Water from the dripping baggie of ice trickled off her forehead.

Mrs. Foster was at her usual place by the door as we arrived at school the next morning. Children and moms basked in her predictably cheerful greeting. Seeing the bandage she emoted, "Kari, what happened to your eye?"

"Mommy and Daddy were *fighting!*"

I sputtered an explanation.

"You wouldn't believe all the things the kids tell us," Mrs. Foster replied good naturedly.

29

Doug and Derek soon turned twelve and TWA's offer was too good to resist! "Kids fly free on TWA." We were sure that wonderful educational opportunities awaited us in Washington D.C.

"Neal, we've got to call Kathy. Maybe we can take her out to dinner or something."

Mother Teresa's liaison, now our friend, had visited our home once before. Expectantly I dialed the 206 area code. "Kathy, this is Jeannie Satre in California. We're bringing the boys to Washington for Easter and I hope we can get together."

"Get together!?" Kathy had maintained her New York accent. "Use my house. Use my car. My house is your house!"

"Gee Kathy, all I wanted was a cup of coffee."

Plans were made. But before hanging up, I had to ask, "Hey, is Mother Teresa allowing adoptions in California again?"

Kari and Resa had been the last. Complicated state department mandates discouraged her from continuing in our state.

"Why? Are you interested?"

"Well, yes, someday. But Derek and Douglas say we already have too many girls. If we ever adopt again, I guess its time for a brother."

"Hey. I just happen to have the most fantastic little boy sitting right here on my desk! But I guess he wouldn't work. He's the same age as the twins."

"That doesn't bother me."

"He's had polio and has been in the children's home since he was a baby."

"Mohan" was only six months younger than Kari and Resa. We were already familiar and comfortable with the post-polio condition. And even though we had no real plans to adopt again, we were open to God's leading. After Neal and I conferred, I called back. "Send the picture!"

But didn't we know? Once we saw the picture, our commitment followed? That was historic! Little two-year-old Mohan was no exception. His dark eyes and olive skin gave him an international look. He could be Greek or Italian. His bleak smile made him sweet and vulnerable. Light skin and big ears made him the perfect Indian son....until polio.

Neal and I settled into our favorite booth. Dinner out often provided the ambiance conducive for good discussions. In this case, it was time for decision making. "So, what do you think?" I ignored the menu.

"Well, it would be fun to have a little boy again. He could share Kari and Resa's room. I'll make him a little bed like the girls'." Bunk beds fashioned from crib mattresses helped to make the bedrooms roomier.

"We already know all about surgery and therapy. It sounds like it would work to me."

"You know the kids would love another child, too. They're so willing to share. It's really up to us though, if we think we can handle it. I think we can." Neal had a positive outlook.

It didn't take long to decide that Mohan, whom we'd already named David, would be a wonderful addition to our growing family. Our youth, faith, and the DeBolt's continuing example, made it easy to reach out to a needy child.

God's word encouraged us too, "Let us not become weary in doing good... Therefore, as we have opportunity, let us do good to all people, especially to those who are of the household of the faith" (Galatians 6:9-10).

After *another* home study, the frustration of more delays confronted us. In the meantime, we continued with our trip to Washington D.C. We looked forward to staying at Kathy's, even though they'd be in New York most of the week. House and car privileges were exchanged for babysitting daughter "Aniter's" guinea pig. After one short visit with Kathy's family, we were on our own!

⚜ 30 ⚜

While we continued to wait for David's arrival and addition to our growing family, we got to know Adele, the Pan Am purser who would bring our new son home. She related her story with enthusiasm.

"I was working on Kari and Resa's flight when Debbie brought them home. She told me about volunteering with Mother Teresa. I love India! Now I get as many flights there as I can."

Adele's visits helped document David's adoption with beautiful color photos of him in Delhi. Lorna, a British volunteer, became David's special friend. Her first letter gave us an idea of our son's personality.

Dear Family Satre,
Mohan is a sweet natured boy. He always greets me with a smile and puts his arms out to be picked up. He loves to be cuddled! He is very active and gets around the floor but can't cope with stairs. He doesn't speak any English but happily repeats any words I say to him. He has had no schooling and can't count or do any other of the basic school lessons but loves to look at books and likes the idea of learning.
He was fascinated with his family photos and gifts. The name David was fun since my son is called David and Mohan thought it a great idea to have the same name. My David is 4 years old and sometimes goes with me to the orphanage so Mohan knows him. The back page is Mohan's!
Yours,
Lorna

She often spent time with him at the children's home and kept us informed on his progress.

Dear Family Satre,
Here we are with our latest combined effort! Mohan has not had much practice at using colours and the results aren't very wonderful, but I wish you could see how seriously he sits and colours to write to you all! He is never tired of looking at his post from you. The soap was rapidly used up of course but everything else is still in tact. He is especially pleased with the mirror and spends ages sitting looking at himself!...
I must mention that at the time when I walked in to talk to him for this letter the children had just been given huge chunks of watermelon by a visitor (delicious in this heat). Mohan immediately put his down and said he'd rather write to you! I had to reassure him that there was no hurry and that he could eat his watermelon first! That's all for this time!
Yours,
Lorna

In Lorna's words, "Inevitably the time of waiting ahead will be a difficult one for everyone concerned and I try to be of help in passing that time usefully." She was a great help to us and her letters were always encouraging.

Hopefully, pictures of us and our house would help David's adjustment as it had with Mindy. Getting the children acquainted with our pets was always important. Dogs in India and Korea are often rabid. Children there are *taught* to be fearful.

"What did David think when he saw the picture of Bear?" Doug laughed. Our big white German Shepherd could look intimidating.

With eight of us to greet him, David's arrival was an exciting family affair! Lingering at the airport while he played with his new toys, eased the transition. Neal and I hung on each of Adele's words as she described the details of their exhausting journey.

"I don't think David even knew he was on an airplane. I'll bet he thought we were just in a big room. How could he understand?" More stories followed of their night in a New York hotel. "When we got on the plane today, he became real pensive." With David and baby Preema to care for, Adele was busy!

Our conversation was suddenly pierced, "Wah-ah-ah-ah." Kari was inconsolable. She was indignant to be the recipient of David's whack.

"Oh, Kari, it's all right. You were only trying to help, but David thought you were taking his toy. He doesn't understand." Stirrings of resentment colored her impression of her new brother.

With both of David's legs limp due to Polio, he was the type of child I expected when we got Mindy. My first challenge was again the airport bathroom. Awkwardly, I juggled belt, zipper and jeans. While desperately trying not to drop him, I encouraged him with smiles and Hindi bathroom words. "Su, su?" Dressing was later simplified with elastic waists and *no belts!*

We all knew that a person is not his handicap, but getting to know and love David personalized it. Knowing the whole person, we focused on what *he could do* rather than on his limitations.

David's crawling became normal to us. Light and agile, he easily scrambled up into chairs and vacant laps. Our few Hindi words proved to be helpful in our day-to-day routine.

The three "little kids" had a great time playing and David was all set for pre-school when the girls went back to their four-year-old class. David attended a class for three-year-olds at the school next door. Mothers hushed their children as I carried David to his class. "There's the boy who can't walk!"

Even the teachers disappointed me. Why point David out to the children as he crawled to the drinking fountain? Couldn't they treat him like the other three-year-olds? I joined the ritual of waiting for class dismissal with clusters of moms crowded around each door.

"Mrs. Satre? Could you wait a minute?" asked his teacher. David and I lingered watching kids match up with moms and rush off.

"I thought it might be helpful if you could go home and write down all of the words David can say in English."

Was she kidding? Did she feel he wasn't progressing? I tried to mask my hostility, "Well, he's only been here for *two months*. I'm not really concerned about his English. I talk to him and someday he'll talk back. If he isn't speaking English after a year, then I'll worry." Our other children learned by imitation and I was sure David would too.

"Well, I just thought you might...." she continued.

"Listen, as a mother of seven, I don't have the time or desire to follow anyone around recording their words. It's like when the Doctor asks me the state of their stools. I don't know that either!" Did I shock her?

But she wouldn't let up, "Oh David, you are so lucky to live in the U-nit-ed S-tates of A-mer-ica. Look at our flag. It is so-o-o special." This information seemed a bit premature for a three-year-old who couldn't speak or understand English. Although she meant well, I thought she was out of touch!

Fortunately, David didn't comprehend the situation. Impending surgery and Christmas vacation provided a graceful break from school. I felt they were also relieved to be rid of their "problem."

Our trip to Washington, D.C. with the boys the previous year provided us with a plethora of educational activities. But while visiting Kathy she cornered me, "I need you to contact a family in California who are interested in a post-polio boy from India. Oh, they've adopted before, but never a child with medical needs. You could give them an idea of what to expect."

Eagerly, I attempted to encourage the Dailey's the way Elsie and Dorothy had encouraged me. While they pondered their decision, a wonderful photo arrived in the mail. "Isn't this the cutest kid you've ever seen?" It was their child.... Emmanuel.

Rushing home from the hospital, I handed out tacos around the table. David's surgery was scheduled the next morning. With six children at home and David at John Muir Hospital, I didn't have the time or patience to take a phone call. So I grabbed the receiver reluctantly. "Jeannie, this is Kathy. I just can't believe it. All the hard to place children have families *except* Emmanuel."

"What happened to the California family?"

"They're not going to take him. They don't have good medical care. And the only therapist in their small town hates kids. So they've said no. I've placed the whole list of twenty kids, except him." I let her continue. "I've even placed a blind girl who screams all the time. Emmanuel isn't that difficult. I told the 'sisters' that *I* would take him, but they won't let me. They say he's too handicapped for me. Do you have any ideas?"

With David's surgery foremost in our minds, I made no promises. Although it had been love at first sight for me when I saw Emmanuel's picture, I was sure Neal would need quite a bit of convincing. But Emmanuel wasn't without a family for long! As a friend said later, "You finally got the hint that he was meant to be your little boy." I knew she was right!

A shorter home study updated our records. By this time the social workers were our friends and they, in turn, admired and respected our family. But now that Derek and Douglas were twelve, Nadine decided to talk to them alone. "I need to ask them how they feel about having one more sibling."

Later we received a glowing report, "You know why all this works don't you? It's because of your boys." Maybe she overstated it, but Derek and Doug's enthusiasm and positive attitude provided good examples for the younger children to emulate.

"It's important that they know they'll have to share their inheritance." Although Nadine was serious, Neal and I laughed uproariously to ourselves. At the rate we were going we didn't need to worry about our financial portfolio!

31

Hip contractures and surgery. We'd done this before! But David's new doctor had a different procedure. "He'll be in the hospital two nights. Then a spika cast for two and a half months. It won't be difficult," the doctor explained.

What a relief not to have the long hospitalization Resa had. David was a trooper, but the spika cast provided its own challenges. Hard white plaster stretching from the top of his waist to the tip of his toes, a piece of broom handle kept his legs apart. We hefted David everywhere he could fit and our Toyota hatch back provided perfect transportation. A mechanics dolly, our neighbor's suggestion, was a lifesaver! Lying on his tummy David scooted on the dolly all around the house *and pre-school*!

What a difference the new school made! His huge cast and scooter board didn't daunt the director's enthusiasm. Mrs. Foster was gifted. She treated him like any other three year old and I'll always be grateful for her matter of fact, loving attitude. David was popular and the other children anxiously waited to try out his scooter board.

The casts were followed by long-legged metal braces with shoes attached. David stood for the first time with a tiny aluminum walker. Then came the very fine balance and coordination required to walk with crutches and braces. Our eyes were damp with tears while we watched David triumph over this challenge. Standing for the first time was followed by his perseverance in learning to walk.

"Go David! You can do it!" Our whole family cheered him on. Learning from the DeBolt's, we encouraged independence. So, from the beginning, David put his braces on and dressed himself. We expected the kids to do all they could for themselves.

With surgery, casts, braces, and crutches, I also relied on Elsie's encouragement. Her kids had experienced it all before, and she prepared me for just what to expect. While sharing the same doctors and physical therapists, her guidance was invaluable. In turn, I was able to prepare the children. Her solace increased my confidence in the doctors, hospital, surgery and in the results. She'd been through it so I guess I could handle it too! Without Elsie's family and the DeBolt's example, our adoptions might have been fewer and less medically involved. This was a powerful example to us of how God uses people in our everyday lives.

Without limits, our children strive at their own pace to accomplish their interests. David is very strong in the upper body and constantly surprises people with his physical prowess. At twelve he joined a canoeing class through the Red Cross with a goal of earning a merit badge for Boy Scouts.

Walt, the leader, sounded concerned. "Dr. Satre, I'm a little worried. The kids have to dump the boats and get back in by themselves. Won't that be hard for David?"

"No problem. The strength of his arms definitely makes up for his limp legs." He was first to pop right back into the canoe!

Wheelchair basketball is his passion! The boys are also enthusiastic band members and keep our house jumping with trumpet sounds and drum rhythms! Resa was a cheerleader at her high school and nothing seems to stop any of the children when it's something they want to do.

32

In the middle of our home study for Stephen, another more serious matter weighed heavily on my mind. Learning the truth about my birth forced me to deal with my biological family's breast cancer history. Suddenly I realized that these dreaded genes were now my own. Vowing not to be fearful like my mother had been, I became calmly diligent in my check ups.

Apprehensive women of various ages lined the walls of Dr. Wright's office. The stale air and cramped quarters gave us all a claustrophobic feeling, but at thirty-seven, the prospect of a second mammogram left me obliviously unconcerned. After enduring the mild discomfort and embarrassment of the exam, I went back to my "McCall's." Impatiently, I flipped through the pages as I waited for the doctor to read my x-ray. Nothing had prepared me for the emotional time bomb I'd soon experience!

Dr. Wright entered with my pictures clutched in his hand. "Jeanne, its good news. Your breasts have not changed much since the last exam." My shoulders slumped in premature relief. "But you are full of dense fibrous tissue we call Fibrocystic Disease. Because of this, and considering your family history, I think you should have an operation." Anxiously I anticipated what he might say next. "It's call a subcutaneous mastectomy, and I think you should have it. I'll send my report to Dr. Davis and you can discuss it with him." Before I could collect my thoughts, he turned and was gone.

His very dogmatic *"should have"* shocked and traumatized me. Now I could barely recall his brief and hurried explanation. I remembered only that my breast tissue would be removed. Vaguely familiar with the operation, I also realized that it was controversial.

Somewhat panicky, I sought the reassurance and guidance of my family doctor who knew me so well. I was sure Dr. Davis would bring me the balance and comfort I sought. I wanted to understand what I was facing before sharing the news with Neal.

"I'm sorry, Dr. Davis is out of town for the next two weeks."

"Out of town!!?? Two weeks??" My shrill response displayed my distress.

So I turned to the American Cancer Society. Surely they could give me information and solace. "Hello. I need you to help me. The radiologist just told me I need to have a subcutaneous mastectomy and my doctor is out of town. I wonder if you could tell me if the Cancer Society has an opinion about the operation. I need some guidance."

"We have no stand about that." The brusk voice left me feeling disappointed and angry. I continued, "But, this is really difficult. The doctor wants me to have this very extensive surgery. I don't know what to think. I'm perfectly healthy."

"*Everyone* who finds out they have cancer has been perfectly healthy," she sniffed. "You'll just have to talk to your doctor." Disbelieving and defeated I slowly hung up the phone. Neal reassured me with a cautious wait and see attitude.

"Don't worry until you talk to Dr. Davis." I wasn't really worried about losing my chest. From the age of ten I'd had an ample bust and even before that I'd stuffed the 28 AA's with toilet paper. As a girl I endured the snickers of the boys in my neighborhood. So I'd never longed for big breasts. But I did wonder about the surgery and especially what *pain* would be involved.

Before long, a flood of people, information, and open doors helped me make one of the most crucial decisions in my life. Neal's secretary had the same surgery years before.

Then two more "friends of friends" listened to my myriad of questions. "How painful was the surgery? What about recovery? How had their relationship with their husbands been affected? Were there complications to the implants? "*Not painful,*" was the term I seized and remembered. "Your nerves are cut so it really isn't that bad." I guessed I could handle it... they had.

Candid conversations with these women who'd had the surgery helped me. Each of them had the same procedure for the same reason: overwhelming family cancer histories and dense breasts. Early detection would be difficult.

Even *Good Housekeeping* screamed:

"Breast surgery to *prevent* cancer: the big dispute. The cruel choice lies between needless surgery and possibly needless loss of life....Many surgeons perform what is called a subcutaneous mastectomy. In this operation, an incision is made under each breast...then 85-95 percent of breast tissue is removed...In the same or a later operation, reconstruction is done with preshaped breast implants....Dr. John Woods of Mayo Clinic feels that prophylactic mastectomies are justified by statistics on the occurrence of breast cancer in the high risk patients he has seen. Without mastectomy, this group has a 10-50 percent chance of getting breast cancer. The risk after the operation is reduced to 0.2 percent."[5]

Zealously, I seized and pondered the vital information. More than once, I heard discussions of "my operation" over the car radio. Dr. Edele's voice was earnest, "A free genetic study is available for women who've had two or more close relatives die of breast cancer. Call Dr. Patricia Kelly at the San Francisco Regional Cancer Foundation."

Instinctively, I knew it was time to take charge of my own research and investigation. This was an *important* step. While waiting for my appointment day, "Getting Breast Cancer - A Look at the Odds" grabbed my attention in the S.F. Chronicle. Under the banner headline a photo of *Dr. Patricia Kelly* stared out at me! Hungry for any shred of information, I started to read:

> "The mysterious connection between heredity and breast cancer still puzzles medical science, but enough is already known to offer those women and thousands of others a reasonable estimate of the risks they may run in developing the disease when cancer has already struck in their immediate family...
>
> Very occasionally, so-called 'prophylactic' surgery in a high-risk patient where cancer is not yet evident has actually turned out to have removed a 'hidden' tumor – still so tiny it could not be detected by conventional means...
>
> 'What really relieves people's anxiety,' she says 'is knowing everything that anyone knows about heredity, and risk factors and probabilities–complete with all the uncertainties.'
>
> In her work Kelly offers no medical advice; she does not counsel 'prophylactic' surgery for those at high risk, nor anything like total security for those at low risk."[6]

The day I was waiting for came at last. I maneuvered my van through familiar San Francisco avenues with ease and arrived at the S.F.Public Health offices early. Set against a sapphire sky and soft billowy cumulus clouds, the historic wood frame complex looked warm and welcoming. I prayed for God's guidance as I trudged up the grassy knoll toward the entrance. Anxiously, I entered Dr. Kelly's office. Surely she would make sense of my confusing situation and give me the confidence I needed to determine my future.

"Hi! You must be Jeanne. I'm Patricia Kelly." She took my hand. Her down to earth manner and quiet friendliness put me immediately at ease.

"I hope you can help me. Several women in my family died at forty. I have seven children, really almost eight, and I want to live to raise them." A mother herself, she patiently listened to my enthusiastic ramblings about my family.

Then she intervened, "We need to investigate your whole family. I have several pages of questions for you to answer. Any medical or death records that you can obtain will help us immeasurably. After we put all of this information together, I can be more specific. I'll give you an evaluation of your chances of contracting breast cancer. But," she continued, "I won't be able to tell you whether or not to have the operation." I was beginning to realize that the final decision would be mine alone.

Looking at my birth mother's records was a wrenching experience for me. I vividly remembered Eleanor's illness and hospitalization. Pale and fragile, she put up a valiant fight. Now the ominous scientific words of her suffering hit me hard and left me trembling.

Death: September 1, 1957, 9:15 a.m.
Autopsy: September 1, 1957, 12 noon
Clinical Summary: This is the first U.C.H. admission for this 39 year old, white, married female on May 27, 1957. During a pregnancy in 1952, a left breast lump was found and a radical mastectomy for carcinoma was undertaken at Franklin Hospital.....The patient did well until 1956 when a right simple mastectomy was performed because of right breast carcinoma. She then was able to carry on at home until six weeks prior to admission here, when she developed severe low back and right hip

pain, which at first appeared periodically but just prior to admission was constant. During this time, she had also become very anorexic and weak, and easily fatigued.
Family History: Sister and mother died of carcinoma of the breast.
Clinical Impression: breast carcinoma, metastatic to lumbar spine, pelvis and lungs."

Between these lines were laboratory findings that Dr. Kelly found significant.

Searching my memory, I remembered my young cousin Bill's cancer of the jaw. I was a child at the time he was ill, but my recall would provide relevant information regarding a soft tissue tumor. Young and blond, he died in his thirties after having radical facial surgery and enduring tremendous suffering. Although these incidents would merely be case histories to Dr. Kelly, they'd always remain significant family members to me.

With the study completed, Neal came with me to hear the news. We wanted to do the reasonable thing....but *what* was that? From the beginning, preserving my life was paramount in our minds. I was being given an opportunity to alter the course of my medical history. Still, it was a controversial operation.

"...surgery without signs of breast cancer is unconventional, and since breast removal, more than any other surgical procedure, can have severe psychological effects, prophylactic mastectomy has drawn bitter criticism from many doctors."[7]

Neal assured me of his love for me. Breasts or no breasts, his love would remain the same. I made lists of the pro's and con's, but medical help would be vital in deciding.

Dr. Kelly's demeanor remained calm and confident as she related the information, "Your chances came out 'one in two' or fifty percent." How I wished I could discern what she was thinking, but there were no clues in her voice or body language. "As I told you before, I can't advise you, Jeanne. That isn't my role, but I'd suggest that you go to U.C. Medical Center for an opinion. I'll recommend a radiologist and a surgeon for you to see. They're both renowned in their fields and I think they'll give you some good guidance." *Finally*, I began to feel like I had something to go on.

I entered U.C.S.F. as a potential patient rather than as a dental wife. Fifteen years earlier this had been our neighborhood. Now a huge university parking garage cut into the whole Arguello hill where our apartment had stood. Even my mother had lived there in the '30's! This had been a famous hill, the steepest in the city. Hundreds of steps in the sidewalk provided hardy pedestrians with a route to Parnassus Street.

Deja vu continued to distract me as I applied for a U.C. Clinic card. My mammograms, previously lost in the mail, were presently clutched securely under my arm. Emerging from the elevator I was awestruck by the expanse of glass and unexpected panorama of "the city." My eyes swept beyond Lone Mountain, Temple Emmanuel, the Presidio, and on out to the Golden Gate Bridge and San Francisco Bay. The crisp sunshine and scenic atmosphere helped me approach my appointment with optimism.

However, I shouldn't have been so excited to see the radiologist. Tall and lanky, he slid into the examining room with x-rays in hand. Without a greeting he immediately laid it out, "What bothers you more, dying of cancer or losing your breasts?" Devastated, I stared at him in blank disbelief. Couldn't he have even said "hello" first!? "After reviewing your mammogram and health history, I would say that you don't have a choice." I had hoped for direct guidance, but this wasn't really what I wanted to hear.

An appointment with Dr. Hunter followed. I was grateful that Neal came with me again. Nervously, we waited in the tiny cubicle for the eminent surgeon to arrive. Still wearing his scrub greens, Dr. Hunter created a larger than life presence, but he seemed thoroughly exhausted. Both his shoulder and left arm drooped to the side as he spoke, "Jeanne, you're in a tough spot. The choice is really up to you. As I see it, you could have the surgery. You could have it either here or in Walnut Creek. The hospital stay would be about five days with no lifting for seven weeks due to the implants. Your other choice, which is just as viable, is to get frequent mammograms and be followed carefully by a physician. That way we'd hope to spot a beginning cancer." *'Hope to spot'* was the key phrase to me. There would be no guarantees.

Either/or!!! Surgery or frequent mammograms! Neal and I left the clinic depressed and confused. How could I chart my course when the medical community couldn't even agree?

"He seems great, but I wouldn't want him to do surgery on me. I'm not sure he could stay awake." We laughed at Neal's sick humor!

We didn't feel like going right home, so we settled for dinner at Pier 39. The picture post card Bay view at "Neptune's Palace" gave us time to review my alternatives. We had so much to 'process.' After exhausting every possible angle, we needed a change. Goldie Hawn, on the big screen, gave me the lift I needed. "I want to go to lunch! I want to wear sandals" she whined. I, like 'Private Benjamin,' longed for simpler and more frivolous times.

Neal, attentive and tender, endured my repetitive barrage of questions. But it was still ME!... my body, my history, my life and my decision. The ominous black cancer cloud hovered menacingly above my head. There was no way I could ignore that fact. "Neal, I'll really kick myself if I refuse the surgery and have cancer in a few years, but, maybe I'll be fortunate and be spared." I was torn between the alternatives.

Frequently I tossed and turned while Neal snoozed peacefully beside me. In the dark loneliness of the night I often reached for my Bible. God never failed to meet me with the encouragement and guidance I so desperately longed for.

> "Therefore, since we have been justified through faith, we have peace with God through our Lord Jesus Christ, through whom we have gained access by faith into this grace in which we now stand. And we rejoice in the hope of the glory of God. Not only so, but we also rejoice in our sufferings, because we know that suffering produces perseverance; perseverance, character; and character, hope. And hope does not disappoint us, because God has poured out his love into our hearts by the Holy Spirit, whom he has given us." (Romans 5:1-5).

Familiar verses like Romans 8:28 resounded in my mind, "And we know that in all things God works for the good of those who love him, who have been called according to his purpose." And Philippians 4:6-7, "Do not be anxious about anything, but in everything, by prayer and petition, with thanksgiving, present your requests to God. And the peace of God, which transcends all understanding, will guard your hearts and your minds in Christ Jesus."

Still, I had more avenues to pursue. An oncologist at John Muir Hospital concurred with the others' opinions... surgery or diligent follow-up. His wife was choosing frequent mammograms, but she didn't have eight *young* children!

Neal leaned toward surgery but was leery of silicone implants. "Who needs implants?" Three preschoolers and David's crutches and braces wouldn't facilitate *seven weeks* of no lifting! "Why not a simple mastectomy? Go see Dr. Andrews and let's get this over with." Indecision was beginning to wear on both of us.

Dr. Andrews, my dad's surgeon, was familiar with our family and his warm fatherly greeting reassured me. I knew I was in caring and competent hands. "I want to get on with my life. How about a simple mastectomy? It's practical and the recuperation time is reasonable."

His response surprised me, "Jeannie, you are much too young and attractive a woman not to have breasts. If you were my wife, I'd recommend silicone implants." I couldn't believe it! Was this a medical or a male opinion?

Several things contributed to what I finally owned as my choice. Foremost in my mind was my responsibility as mother. When Dr. Davis' wife accidentally discovered a large invasive tumor he was convinced. "Carol had just had a clear mammogram. She discovered the tumor, the size of a lemon. I'm just worried that a beginning cancer would be masked by your dense breast tissue." He also insisted on implants.

So, after nine months of research, Neal and I conferred with the plastic surgeon. He showed us before and after photos and we set up a date... a double mastectomy with immediate silicone implants placed under the chest muscle wall. I was also aware that a cancer could possibly be found during the operation. Despite his surgical expertise, Dr. Moore's lack of warmth and communication concerned me.

Fortunately, his secretary exhibited the emotional support that he failed to provide. Her sincere encouragement and mental preparation for surgery was invaluable to me. So the die was cast! To delay any longer would only have lengthened the agony of our inevitable decision.

33

A Southern California vacation immediately preceded my hospital date. It was just what our whole family needed! Sailing out of Balboa Bay on the Davies' yacht relaxed me at once. Refreshing sea air washed over my face and replaced my tension with a feeling of well being. The four older kids enthusiastically bounced all over the deck and scurried down below for cold Cokes. Passing the homes of John Wayne and Buddy Epsen left us northerners star struck.

After dinner at the Davies' beach house, our memorable day at sea came to a close. We couldn't believe our overnight accommodations at the palatial "Newporter Hotel." Conscious of not disturbing our "neighbors" with raucous kid noises, I kept our TV and comments at a whispered level. Everyone was tucked in and joyful with anticipation of our next day's visit to Disneyland, as Neal and I switched off the lights. Typically, *I* was the one to toss and turn!

At *1:30 a.m.* our neighbors slammed into their room and the TV blasted! The pillow over my head didn't stifle the noise and neither did the toilet paper that I gingerly stuffed into my ear canals. None of my roommates stirred as I fumed with anger at this inconsiderate behavior.

How could they sleep? Suffering with frustration, I fantasized my revenge. "We have to get up at 7a.m. Surely, they plan to sleep in. What if someone inadvertently reversed the 'Do Not Disturb' sign that dangled from their doorknob?" I wondered. "Would the maid be prompt in cleaning their room?"

But my imaginings came to an abrupt halt as the Space Shuttle countdown reverberated through the wall. "They'll never turn it off now!" So I called the desk, "The people next door have their TV blasting and now the Space Shuttle has come on. Could you please ask them to turn it off?"

Self satisfied, and wishing I'd called sooner, I waited to hear their phone ring. Instead, their was a soft knock at *our* door. Cracking the door, I pointed in the direction of the culprits. Was this a movie, or was there really a house detective *in a trench coat* at my door at 3 a.m.? What mattered was that this bizarre scene resulted in blissful *silence*.

Just as I rolled over I heard a whirring sound in the hall. Overcome with curiosity I peaked out the door and saw what I had dreaded....a man vacuuming the rugs!

Immediately after returning from our Spring vacation I headed in for my lab tests. Just like Mindy, I dreaded the blood test most. Derek and Doug met me with sheepish grins as I returned from the hospital. Entering the kitchen, a sparkling floor and a giant bouquet of flowers greeted me. One had mopped while the other rode his bike downtown to get the flowers. I was overcome and they loved it!

Covered with prayer and expectant of how God would use this experience, I checked into John Muir Hospital. How I dreaded having to be there alone the night before while feeling perfectly fine. While donning the flimsy hospital gown I was struck with the finality of my surgical decision. Tomorrow morning I would have my breasts surgically removed in a 5 hour operation. There was no turning back. I knew also that, in a number of these operations, a beginning cancer was often found.

Anxiously, we waited for the anesthesiologist. Wasn't he really the most important one? Would I get the doctor I had requested? A knock on my door preceded the doctor's entry. I cheerfully greeted him with, "Hi! You must be Dr. Mc Ewin."

"Uh, no. I'm Dr. Werner."

Good grief! Not only was it the wrong doctor, but this guy was on crutches! But his friendly demeanor quickly won me over and his medical throughness inspired my confidence.

"Oh, well that's fine. But can you stand up for five hours?"

"Sure. Besides, I have a stool."

"Five hours is a long time! Can you send out for a milkshake?" Unlike my surgeon, he seemed to appreciate my humor. So, of course, I liked him.

When Neal finally prepared to leave I savored the warmth of his embrace. I wished that he could stay just a little longer. My feeling of loneliness didn't last long though. The nurse began telling me about the Scottish lady next door. Pulling my pink robe around me I dashed to her room. Could this be the answer to my prayer? Did God really bring a special person for me to encourage in the hospital?

Hearing her magical Scottish brogue excited me and simultaneously brought me comfort. She sounded just like my "Granny Annie" in Edinburgh! Far from home, while visiting cousins, this poor lady's intestine ruptured. Surgery, coupled with a slow recovery, left her feeling lonely and discouraged. But within minutes we were prattling on about Edinburgh and where *my* cousins lived and the places I had visited there. For a brief time at least, our concerns vanished and we were left with the warm glow of friendship.

Back in my private room, I pulled out the note from Mrs. Bender that I had saved for just this moment. Comforting and encouraging scripture references filled her rose covered card. And as I looked up and copied each verse, I was reassured over and over of God's love and care for me. I especially clung to these words from Psalm 91:

> "I will say of the Lord, 'He is my refuge and my fortress, my God in whom I trust....' If you make the Most High your dwelling - even the Lord who is my refuge- then no harm will befall you, no disaster will come near your tent. For He will command his angels concerning you to guard you in all your ways; they will lift you up in their hands, so that you will not strike your foot against a stone. 'Because he loves

me,' says the Lord, 'I will rescue him; I will protect him; I will be with him in trouble, I will deliver him and honor him. With *long life* will I satisfy him and show him my salvation'" (emphasis added).

"My surgery was scheduled for Good Friday. Was I really sharing a very small part of Jesus' suffering? It was meaningful to me. Anyway, I knew that my sides were about to be pierced too. Despite the factual reality, I slept like a baby that night. Not a hint of a "butterfly" entered my mind or body as I was rolled into the operating theater. "100, 99, 98, 97....." I was out!

What turned into *seven and a half hours* of surgery only seemed like minutes to me. Back in my room, late afternoon shadows danced across my wall. Could the day be over already? Neal's presence, holding my hand, was all the communication I could muster. "Jeannie," Neal whispered, "It took longer than they thought. They had to give you a pint of blood. Everything went well though. I'll stay here. Just rest." With the IV hanging over my head and drains coming out of both my sides, I could only lie still. Slight jaundice shaded my face.

Soon a disgustingly cheerful aide intruded on my drug induced solitude. "Here's your dinner honey!"

I could understand some clear broth, but did they really think I could attempt a stuffed bell pepper smothered in tomato sauce? Just the sight of it made me call for my little plastic trough!

As I became more lucid, Neal explained the day. "They did everything as planned. The implants are under your chest muscle wall and he did some delicate work too. I think that's why it took so long. There wasn't any apparent cancer, but there will be lab tests. Dr. Moore seemed satisfied." With ace bandages binding my chest like a tube top, I had no sense of what I looked like. But I knew what I felt.

Not expecting a painful operation, I wondered why I had the crushing weight of a Mack truck on me. I lived for my pain shots and feared the day I would be weened to pills.

"Dr. Moore, promise that I can have a pill when I need it. I'm really worried about the transition." At the same time I rejoiced that my pathology tests were clean. But there was no explanation about the searing pain. He reassured me about the pills and left abruptly.

Elsie's afternoon visit lifted my spirits. With discomfort and a fever, my hospital stay lengthened. As we chatted, my agony returned. Calling for the nurse, I anticipated the capsules the doctor had promised.

But this nurse went by the book! "You're not due for a pill for another hour," she announced and turned on her heels. I rang my bell again. "Dr. Moore said I could have as much medication as I needed and I *need*..." In frustration, I succumbed to a flood of tears.

So Elsie intervened. "What she's saying is that she's hurting and she needs a pill NOW!!" And I got it! From then on I remembered Alice as my "mean nurse."

꧁ 34 ꧂

After seven days, I returned home. Despite my fever in the hospital, it wasn't until my first post operative doctor's visit that they discovered the reason for my pain was....a raging staph infection! But my chest looked pretty good to me and I looked forward to having "perky" breasts. The doctor pointed out a little bubble forming on one side, like a weakness on a tire. Armed with antibiotics I headed home to my place on the couch. My orders were no lifting for seven weeks. And I still couldn't drive.

Car-pools and food from friends and church members saved our days! With three pre-schoolers, I *attempted* resting! My next doctor's visit revealed the bad news, "That bubble's bigger! It's a sign of the infection. We don't have any choice but to remove the implant on that side. We can do it in day surgery."

The thought of another operation depressed me! I didn't want implants in the first place. Neal and I entered the elevator heading to the day surgery area. As the door opened, a young woman with the largest breasts we'd ever seen joined us. We escaped at our floor groaning in fits of laughter. "What timing!"

With thirteen shots of novocaine in my arm pit, I felt no pain. Focusing on the background music and the surgical nurse's encouraging words made it bearable. It wasn't long before the implant was removed and I was lop-sided. Now I had open wounds that needed irrigation and medication. Neal took care of me without a flinch.

Before long the other side began to bubble. I prayed that this wasn't happening again. The weak area grew so fast that the implant began to pierce my flesh. On my next office visit the doctor "delivered" it through my skin. With so many severed nerves this procedure didn't even hurt. But now, in place of my new chest, I had deep open wounds and keloids forming on my numerous scars.

Putting up a brave and optimistic front, I chose the shower to deal with my new body. My tears flowed. All the doctor talked about was when he could operate again. "We'll have to wait about a month, but then we can just re-do it all." He had to be kidding! He'd taken my "before" picture, but declined the "after." Showing no care for me as a whole person, I was treated like a medical failure. Feeling both physically and emotionally fragile, I was left to sort out my disappointment without his professional help.

Over and over I repeated my thoughts and 'what ifs' to Neal. As usual, I processed every thought through my mouth and he always listened. "I know I've said this before, but...." My adjustment took months.

Neal was adamant, "I don't want you going through anymore surgery! If you need to do it for you, o.k. But don't do it for me. I just want you to heal and put this all behind us."

I totally agreed. Recovery overshadowed my feelings of deep disappointment. How I wished I had stuck with what I'd asked for in the first place...a simple mastectomy. "From now on I'll 'buy' my boobs!"

As I healed, I improvised with socks stuffed in my surgical bra. Again I turned to the Cancer Society for help. "I understand that you have a display of different prosthesis possibilities at your office."

And again I was rebuffed by the same crotchety receptionist.* Her voice was like ice, "I don't know about 'display', but we have a list of different dealers." Since I didn't have cancer there was no offer of a "Reach to Recovery" volunteer for me. I was "on my own."

---

*This was an *individual*! Please do not hesitate to contact *your* local American Cancer Society.

Did I really want to be "fitted" in the back room of a pharmacy amid packing boxes and male employees wandering around? Or could I handle "Angelina's" locked shop? *She demanded* that you agree with her choice...what I called a "Brunhilda bra." "You have to get this, otherwise your back will collapse. It goes with your bone structure. That's it!" So I did my own thing awhile longer.

Finally, I remembered seeing Ruth Handlery on TV. As well as creating the "Barbie" doll, she had invented a better prosthesis! With a great sense of humor and *joie de vrie*, she displayed her chest on TV talk shows. She said women should be able to shop for "breasts" in upscale department stores. I thought so too!

So working up my courage, and hoping I didn't run into anyone I knew, I headed for the lingerie dept. in our most prestigious store. "May I help you dear?" hissed the elegant overly dressed saleswoman.

Although intimidated, I faked a confident air. "I'm interested in the 'Nearly Me' prosthesis. I need them for both sides." While shooting me a skeptical look, she reached in the drawer. "Make yourself comfortable in the dressing room dear, and I'll be there in a minute to fit you."

"Comfortable?" She had to be kidding. "Fit me?" Couldn't I just try it on myself? I knew she'd probably faint when she saw my scars, but she kept her composure. I was relieved to see the pretty bras she offered. A former 34C/D I had looked forward to smaller breasts. No more hefty underwires for me! And I wasn't emotionally ready to accept a sturdy mastectomy bra. So I was happy with my choice and, $500. later, I felt like a new woman!

Besides Neal's constant attentiveness and understanding, prayer support and God's strength kept me sane. The black "breast cancer cloud" had been removed. I don't look back. It's not my nature! Besides, I felt divinely led into my decision.

35

I had six months to recover from surgery before welcoming Stephen Emmanuel. What a "character!" He celebrated his arrival by blowing us big smacky kisses at the airport. Dark curls covered his head and at three-and-a-half I was glad he was still little enough to cuddle. Stephen quickly settled in with his three sibling playmates, so close in age. For starters the four "little kids" shared a room with the miniature bunk beds fashioned by Neal. Bath and bedtimes were always riotous and I loved the happy splashing squeals followed by the calmer bedtime story hour.

Stephen's one leg needed straightening but progressive casting did the job...no hospital! What a relief after what we had been through with Resa and David. First he wore a long metal brace on one leg with his shoe attached. And eventually he could walk without it. What a miracle that he only needed a built up shoe. Even his doctor was surprised!

One of the joys we have experienced in adopting children with special needs is seeing them go so far beyond expectations of ourselves and of the doctors. And we're not alone! Many families have similar stories. "Just don't tell the kids what they *can't do!*"

We thought Stephen would always have a long leg brace. Wrong! And when the doctor watched him kick a ball, he mumbled quizzically, "I don't see how he can do that. He doesn't have the muscles!"

Mistakenly Neal told Stephen, "There are so many fun things you'll be able to do but you probably won't ride a bike." What a challenge! The very next day Stephen was riding a bike! From then on both Neal and I kept our mouths shut.

Kids seem to find miraculous ways of achieving the unexpected!

And as Dorothy Debolt says, "Children don't sit and worry about the things they *can't do* because there are so many things that they *can do*, and they're busy doing them!"

Stephen's arrival, only one year after David's, came much closer than any of our other adoptions. I told twelve year old Derek, who seemed to want an Atari (now Nintendo or Sega) more than he wanted another brother... "Don't worry Derek we'll get 8S INUF as our license plate."

"Yeah Mom. Last year was lucky seven, this year's eight is enough, next year you'll say nine is fine." But I kept my word.

And while waiting for Douglas to take his driving test, I achieved my goal..."8S INUF!" But Derek must have sensed what I would learn later.

36

Early in February during Derek and Douglas' senior year in high school, I received another challenging phone call. Hearing from Maureen startled me. "Since you and Neal work with "AASK"[8] I hope you can help me. Rebecca's a teenager with special needs and I need a home for her."

"That's not hard. I'm sure AASK can help," was my confident reply.

"I'm her night time attendant. The family she's living with has to move. We sure don't want her to get put into the 'system.'" Rebecca would have to experience upheaval again.

"We want a *special* home for her." Maureen sounded earnest.

That seemed understandable. But her next stipulation floored me. "We want a Christian home in the Las Lomas School District." She was adamant. "Rebecca's really involved in her school!"

"Las Lomas? Our boy's school? Maybe they know her! So much for AASK!" And who did I *know* who wanted another teenager? That alone would be a lot to ask. But what about a teen in a wheelchair who needs total care? No way! So Maureen and I became phone pals as she educated me about Rebecca.

The Muscular Dystrophy diagnosis surfaced when she was a young child. Now, at seventeen, her mobility depended on an electric wheelchair and help from others. "She can use her right hand," Maureen enthused. "She feeds herself. She can do her homework and even puts on make up by herself!" Our family united in prayer for a home for Rebecca. But it wasn't until our evening coffee date that Neal spilled what was he was thinking, "Have you ever considered Rebecca for us?"

"No, I've never considered Rebecca for us!" That possibility had not even crossed my mind! How scary and confusing. And what about our license plate...8S INUF? That was *my* intention!

BUT GOD! Was He leading us in that direction? There was no doubt. I sensed His tugging and so did Neal. I felt inadequate and scared.

How unusual. Both Derek and Douglas knew Rebecca at school.

"She's really neat, Mom."

"Yeah, neat all right," my mind smoldered. "But that doesn't mean she has to *live* with us."

My conversations with Maureen grew longer while I learned the involvement of Rebecca's daily care. The teen age stage didn't deter me. But I was *very* concerned about how to handle her physically.

"Maureen, that's *total* care! I don't have time to dress and bathe her and take her to the bathroom," I whined. "And what about all that lifting? And someone needs to be with her. What about my life?"

And still God nudged.

Maureen mentioned funding for attendants. Some ways seemed workable. We already had wheelchair ramps. But, in others ways it all sounded beyond us. As Maureen and I talked and talked I related my feelings and doubts to Neal.

"It's really up to you Jeannie. You're the one who'll be most responsible. After all, I go to work!" Still he remained interested and encouraging.

I should have known that going to meet Rebecca in the hospital would be dangerous. With only ten percent lung capacity, pneumonia has always been her frequent enemy.

And now, for the third time this year, Rebecca was in the midst of a serious battle.

But even in her illness, her cheerful and outgoing personality shone through. With many doctors, kids and adult friends in common, we "clicked" right away! And she was even reading one of "my" magazines. Could God use a silly magazine as a "sign?"

From that visit on, I knew. This *was* God's plan. My heart said it was right. But still my emotions dipped and waned. We knew the hospitals, therapy schedules and social workers. Derek and Douglas would be off for college so we would have room.

"Pre-adoptive pregnancy" was rearing its head in my life once more. On a good day I felt invincible. At other times I knew I was totally out of my mind! God would give me the strength but I needed to *be sure*. This was not a task to accomplish on my own power.

My reading soon provided me with a push,

"If we are devoted to the cause of humanity, we shall soon be crushed and broken-hearted, for we shall often meet with more ingratitude from men than we would from a dog; but if our motive is love to God, no ingratitude can hinder us from serving our fellow men."[9]

Our decision needed to be firm before revealing the plan to Rebecca. As far as she knew, I was just a friend of Maureen's. But just as our commitment seemed sure, many of the circumstances changed.

Maureen dropped the news, "Funding for attendants is inadequate. You'll need to hire your own."

"What?" Now she tells me. My mind whirled.

"Try a newspaper ad. And supplement their wages, otherwise no one will answer. Moving day needs to be June 15."

"Great," I thought as I slumped in my chair. Doug and Derek would still be at home.

And Maureen continued, "Rebecca has a big water bed and exercise board. I guess having her own room would be helpful."

"Own room! No one in this family has their own room!"

Her words dashed my resolve to say "yes." Again overwhelmed with doubt and hesitation, my six pros and fifteen cons made the message clear to my logical mind.

37

Disneyland with our four "little kids" gave me the break I needed. How relieved I was that our answer was finally "no." The "Rebecca issue" was behind us. The few days away were free and unpressured. A wonderful time of fantasy and a respite from the needs of the real world.

Then two weeks later, I headed off to the California Women's Retreat. Every year my friends and I anticipated hearing wonderful speakers and having time to visit with other women. What a change the fancy hotel setting was from our day to day lives with young children.

But why did I find myself telling friends about *Rebecca*? That she might come to live with us? I thought it was settled. What was I saying?

Later that night as I made my way through the crowded hall, I spied the prayer basket on a side table. OK! My request...in the basket would put the matter to rest once and for all. Neatly I printed my needs on a small piece of paper... "If God really wants our family to take Rebecca, please make me unconditionally enthusiastic about bringing her into our home." There!

During the weekend God heard my request several times. Women on this prayer committee were serious about their responsibility.

I went home from the retreat refreshed and renewed and amazed at my positive and loving feeling toward Rebecca. Was I really excited and anxious to have her join our family? All of the obstacles I had belabored now seemed insignificant.

Again, as in years past, I called my friend Dorothy DeBolt and she reassured me, "Jeannie, I don't know any family who could do this better than yours. Rebecca is so lucky!" Dorothy had already been through this in her own family. No one could have encouraged me more!

Two weeks later, it was time for Neal and the whole family to meet Rebecca. She and Maureen came for dessert. I was still only a casual friend. Seeing her in her wheelchair for the first time, it struck me how tiny she was.

Sixty-eight pounds of cheerful personality! And what a boisterous time together with each of the children vying to tell her special little tales of their life.

The next day Rebecca cried when Maureen told her we *wanted* her to become part of our family. "How can people with so many kids have room for one more?" she sobbed.

Rebecca had veto power. It was up to her to choose us just as we had chosen her. But now instead of phone conversations with Maureen I chatted with Rebecca. Getting to know each other would surely help with her transition to the lively Satre home.

But now a crisis arose and Maureen called me with pleas for help. Rebecca's date for the Jr. Prom was backing out at the last minute. This was such a special occasion for her. A beautiful dress was being made and she was inconsolable.

The solution seemed immediately clear and again the willingness of our boys came through. "I'll take her Mom," Derek didn't miss a beat. "We'll go to dinner in Berkeley first, then to the dance. It won't be a problem."

Rebecca loved the dances and her seventeen year old social life was spared. But now she says, "It's a good thing I didn't know that Derek would be my brother. Nothing would be worse than going to the Prom with your *own brother!*

Rebecca did everything! If it was "Toga Day" at school, she was "bugging" me for a sheet. She never missed the home games if she could help it. But "dancing" was her favorite. Moving her electric wheelchair to the rhythm of the music, she fully enjoyed the whole "scene." And this was serious.

She *was dancing!* Not "trying" to dance. To treat her in any other way would be condescending.

But Rebecca's situation wasn't always lighthearted. Her former "house parents" painted a potentially grim picture. Their talks with her doctors had revealed that she might not live through her senior year. But from past experience we knew that doctors could be fooled. "Jeannie, only God knows the outcome," urged Neal.

So although we felt somewhat cautious with Rebecca, we weren't discouraged. Our "calling" was to love her and give her a great family. "We'll help her enjoy all the time she has. Whether God gives her days or months or years, she'll have fun here." I concurred with Neal.

Moving day was exciting and the younger kids were especially in gear. Derek was in Japan as an exchange student so the room scarcity was solved. But I was a little apprehensive. Rebecca was coming from a very structured foster home. I hoped our casual but active style would be welcomed.

I needn't have worried. Rebecca thrived and eagerly joined in our family fun, but it wasn't long before she was sick again...serious lung congestion. Now I was initiated into the caregiving role. "Nursing" doesn't come naturally to me, but Rebecca was a good teacher and an appreciative patient.

"Don't worry, I know what to do. I've been taking care of myself for years," Rebecca encouraged.

What a bonding time for us. I sat by her bed and turned her often. Following instructions I pounded her back and helped with her inhaler.

As talkative people, we had no problem relating the stories of our pasts. We really got to know each other during those two weeks. Some of our "stories" were serious...her parent's divorce, my surgery. Others made us laugh and laugh!

"You wouldn't believe the first lady I lived with. She made me pay extra for every little thing I ate. After dinner she'd say, 'Hmmmm, that casserole had chicken and cheese and sour cream in it.' Then she'd tote up the amount I owed." Know-

ing Rebecca's minute appetite made that scene even more
ridiculous.

Now we were jubilant. We kept the pneumonia at bay
and averted a hospitalization. For Rebecca, "the hospital"
became both enemy and deliverer. First we tried avoiding it,
and then we would race to the emergency room praying for
admittance. Rebecca was well known and loved by the staff
who also respected her medical acumen. Understanding all
about blood gasses and oxygen levels, she freely communicated her needs. But amazingly, she always stayed pleasant
and appreciative.

Everyone who knew Rebecca admired her courage and
stamina. We were hooked too! How lucky we were to be a
part of her life. "Rebecca's the first person I've ever met who
really knows how to live one day at a time. What a gift!" Neal
agreed with my pronouncement. "Her attitude has to come
from God."

Although the day to day routine was often physically difficult, all of the girls pitched in to assist. Even nine year old
Kari and Resa helped her dress and bathe. And Mindy soon
became her right hand helper and friend.

In our spontaneous family, the routine had to be flexible. So we took care of Rebecca ourselves and she loved it.
"I'm so glad not to have to go to bed at the same time every
night!"

And many times we joked, "Maureen wouldn't approve
of the late hours you're keeping."

A few weeks after Rebecca joined our family, a line in
our church bulletin caught my eye. "Rebecca, there's a healing service Sunday night at church. I'd love to take you but
it'd be nice if you accepted Jesus into your life first."

Her immediate, "OK what do I do?" astonished me.

I was caught so off guard, it took me a few minutes to
regain my composure. "Now what do I do?" ran through my
mind. But with my hand on Rebecca's we prayed together

asking Jesus to come into her heart to be her Lord and Savior. She was happy and I was walking on air! All of the spiritual seeds that Maureen and her foster family had sown the year before now fully blossomed.

"God's obviously had you in His hands all these years Rebecca. Now you know who to give the credit." She tearfully agreed with me.

So the next Sunday night we entered the candlelit church. "Anyone in need of healing may come up to the front when you're ready. We look forward to praying with you." This was a new experience for our congregation and for us. But we were eager. "OK Rebec, let's go." Neal led the way. The candles flickered and the crowd, accompanied by guitars, sang softly.

Bending over Rebecca, the team leader asked, "What would you like us to pray for?" "Physical health and healing for her lungs," was Neal's whispered reply.

So as the leader put his hand on her shoulder, elderly Mary bent down and put her hand on Rebecca's leg. Suddenly, in this prayerful moment, *Rebecca's wheelchair began to lurch forward.* Mary looked startled and grabbed the chair for balance. But the more she grabbed the more the chair lurched toward her.

This scenario was too much for me. Closing my eyes, I gasped for breath hoping to contain my potential hysteria. And all the while, the candles flickered and the guitar players strummed as the congregation continued to sing softly. Could they even imagine what was going on in front of them?

Rebecca, frantically flailing her right hand, made a vain attempt to reach the power switch on her chair. Then at last, Neal calmly took a hold of Mary's hand and removed it from the smooth round knob she was using for balance...the *same* round knob Rebecca used to drive her chair. After regaining her composure, Mary continued her prayer for health and healing.

Although we still kid her about that evening, God has honored Mary's prayers. Rebecca has endured many more hospitalizations, but her 10% lung capacity has continued to carry her through many more adventures in life. Every day is a miracle...a gift from the Lord!

✦ 38 ✦

Rebecca's senior year was a joyous one. She was the actress in the family. "I really want to major in drama in college. Maybe I can even do movies." And it was "red plate" day when she announced, "You won't believe it. I was chosen to be student director of the fall play!"

Neal and I cringed when she went out to rehearsals in freezing temperatures and stayed out late on school nights. "This isn't conducive to her health," we agreed.

"But, you know Neal, this is her dream. It's the most exciting thing that's ever happened to her." I hoped for his reassurance.

"Jeannie, she's so happy! Even if she dies doing it, how much better than dying in the cocoon of our overprotection." But God is so good and the doctors were wrong! She thrived that year and directed the spring play too.

Right before graduation I heard about "The Extra Effort Award" offered by a San Francisco television news program. "Write in now and tell us about an extraordinary teenager who you feel deserves this honor."

Any letters I write usually stay in the recesses of my mind. But for once I followed through and put my words on paper. And Rebecca won! They televised her receiving the award at a school rally and they filmed her at home with all of us as well. Great excitement!

Graduation soon topped off a wonderful year. Squeals and cheers went up from the bleachers when we heard our girl's name. A diploma would have been satisfying enough, but they were announcing an *award*. "This year 'The Principal's Award' goes to Re-bec-ca Cushing!" Tears of joy and gratitude to God coursed down our cheeks as we witnessed her class of 400 rising to their feet to celebrate Rebecca and her accomplishments.

Our one year commitment of a home for Rebecca stretched to three as she attended Diablo Valley College. Then, following in her brothers' footsteps, she transferred to the University of California. She chose the Davis campus. People would sweetly ask me, "Does she live in a 'home?'"

With a laugh I'd reply, "No, she lives in the dorm with a roommate." Or later, "She lives in a house with friends." Boy, they didn't know Rebecca!

Even with *many* hospitalizations and two horrendous bouts on a respirator in Cardiac Intensive Care, she managed to graduate from college with a degree in Psychology. Watching her proudly motor onto the stage to receive her Bachelor's Degree, Neal and I couldn't help but wonder, "Would her doctors have ever predicted *this?*"

Besides her own accomplishments, we were able to share other special times with Rebecca. Just out of a serious hospital stay, a friend drove her to meet us. "Mom, you know there's no one I'd rather meet than Joni Ereckson Tada. Remember how you read her devotional to me while I was on the respirator?" Joni's books had encouraged me too.

And now the beautiful ranch home was a buzz with excitement. Everyone anticipated the arrival of the courageous Christian woman we all admired. We arrived just before Joni. Then *they* met. Rebecca felt a special connection with this woman in a power chair. They had so much to share. Even without many words we could sense the understanding between them.

As the crowd settled down to listen to the evening's presentation, Conrad pulled Neal and me aside. "The guy who's supposed to start this hasn't shown up. I know that you've experienced a lot as parents. Could you say a few words before Joni speaks?" Wow, that was a lofty invitation. But with many friends in the room and with God's leading, we rose to the occasion.

"We've been blessed to have a wonderful family," I said. "Most of our kids are adopted internationally and many of them are physically challenged. They live very active lives! You know, they can handle their physical problems. But what they can't handle is being treated funny. They want to be included. They want to be invited to the birthday parties. *They* are not their handicaps! They want to be encouraged in what they *can* do. Columnist George Will has a son with Down Syndrome. He says, 'The only thing that separates us from people with disabilities is the rabbit's foot that dangles precariously around our necks.' What if we were in our kids places? Let's follow the example that Jesus gives us and treat physically and emotionally challenged people the way we'd want to be treated."

We received a warm reception. Neal fielded some questions and then it was Joni's turn. She ended her talk with a story that has inspired me ever since. "This year I went to Russia with Billy Graham. At one of the crusades I had a blind interpreter. As the crowds poured into the stadium I described it to him, 'Oh Ivan you should see all the people. There are 60,000 people in a stadium that only holds 30,000.'"

"Then he said, 'It's so curious to me. Why did they choose me, a blind man, to be your interpreter?' And as I watched Billy Graham being helped to the podium, I was in awe. God had chosen a blind young man, a quadriplegic woman in a wheelchair and an old man with Parkinsons's disease to be His messengers." Rebecca, Neal, and I will always remember the impact of that evening with Joni.

We loved having Rebecca live with us; but sometimes it aroused feelings that were often difficult for me to handle. Why couldn't I be more "mature?" We'd never had to "share" a child before.

"We treat her just like our other kids. But why does her Dad get her for special occasions? It's not fair!" Of course, none of this bothered easygoing Neal.

Our family took responsibility for her extensive daily care. We supported her during her numerous hospitalizations. Then every special holiday she was whisked away.

Fortunately, Rebecca and I could talk about it. "I know you're caught in the middle Rebec." It was easier for her to keep them happy. "And no matter what, I know they're still your family." Knowing this was common for foster children, I tried to understand.

I wasn't proud of my hostile feelings, but I couldn't seem to shake them. It took several years before I finally received my answer. It was after her five and a half weeks in Cardiac Intensive Care at Sutter Memorial in Sacramento (a three hour round trip drive for us).

With her temp at 105, and her heart rate at 180, we stayed with her day after day. "This flu bug is going around campus. It's pretty routine. But for Rebecca it's deadly." Dr. Hunt fought for her life, and we put everything on hold. Finally, she got off the respirator...what a grand time of celebration. And then we brought her home!

Three more weeks of recuperation. Never alone, I stayed home with her every day. She needed to regain her strength and continue breathing treatments. Rebecca was a joy to be with, but what about *my life?*

So I whined some more, this time to God. Why do *I* have to do the dirty work?"

The voice might not have been audible, but it was clear to me. The *message* welled up from deep inside of me, "Because I asked YOU to do it, Jeannie!" Rebecca recovered at home, and I was *glad* to take care of her! And that ended the issue for me.

39

Having a family like ours has provided us with some unusual opportunities. One of the most dramatic ones occurred in San Jose, California.

"Jeannie, get rid of that banner!" Neal moaned.

Rolled up beside me sat the winter white butcher paper. A blaze of colorful letters spelled out my heartfelt message, "WE ARE MOTHER'S CHILDREN!" This day had been bathed in prayer as God opened doors step by step. But, in my humanness, I thought maybe He might need a little help from me.

My telephone conversation with Father Lester had instilled an unusual boldness in me. "Father Lester, did you tell Mother about the children?"

"I hope they can meet her. But right now, I'll be lucky just to get the microphone plugged in."

"Well, what shall I do? Should I bring a banner?" How else could she spot us in the San Jose Civic Auditorium? 3,500 people and us!

"Sure. Do whatever you want."

Visions of the savvy politicos who filled the front rows of Mother Teresa's most recent visit stuck in my memory. Surely, she'd rather see "her children." She'd be amazed to see how well they were doing. And maybe, I hoped, she would be encouraged to reinstate her international adoption program. Besides she was a big part of their birth story.

Our well-traveled brown van pulsated with the fervor we all felt as we headed out to meet the Nobel prize winner who had become a mentor to our family. Our children felt she was their friend, "Mommy Teresa" to them! After all, they wrote her letters and sent their birthday money to other children in India.

"You guys look great!" I said enthusiastically as I bathed our four youngest children with my adoring gazes. This was a continuation of the miracle that began years before with their adoption from India.

My thoughts wandered: "Four young children released to the orphanage at birth. Kari and Resa, twin newborns now age eight...David and Stephen, malnourished infants now healthy six and seven year olds. Had their Polio affliction played a role in their relinquishment?"

Remembering the years of red tape and frustration involved in the adoption and immigration procedures, I thrilled at seeing them today...beautiful, healthy and happy members of our large (nine children!) enthusiastic family.

Giddy chatter emanating from the back seats pierced my reverie. Winding through five o'clock commute traffic wracked my nerves. We had come so far since hearing an announcement about this day on the car radio. We couldn't be late!

"This is it Neal. Take this off ramp." A massive construction site appeared before us. "I can't believe this!"

"No problem." Neal kept his characteristic cool as he dropped us off right in front of the Civic Center Auditorium.

All I saw was the concrete mountain of stairs that rose at our feet. But they were *empty*! "Thank you Lord," I breathed. "Come on, let's go!" Holding hands, we started our struggle, step by step, up to the double doors. "Come on, we can do it!" Despite crutches and braces, even little David finally met the challenge.

Breathless, I showed the policeman our tickets.

"Well, you know you have to get in line."

"But we have reserved seats!"

"So do *they*." He gestured to a bank of humanity that snaked around the building.

"But I have all these little kids!"

"Well, O.K. Go on in."

"Thank you again, Lord." The children settled eagerly into the front row. Neal joined me and we sat behind them. Still I fingered the banner and roll of Scotch tape.

"Jeannie, we're in the front row. We don't need the banner!" Neal laughed.

The lady behind me grabbed my shoulder, "I'm the one from the church office who gave you Father Lester's phone number!"

Directly in front of us teemed reporters and cameramen from every conceivable Bay Area station. Eight-year-old Kari carefully held our treasured black and white photo...Mother Teresa holding her as an infant. The same photo that now hangs on the children's home wall in Delhi.

"Is that a picture of you with Mother Teresa? Can you show it to the television camera?" Suddenly floodlights and lenses pointed in the direction of *my* daughter. A microphone was shoved to her mouth.

What would she say? I wondered. *I sure couldn't help her!*

"Kari Satre of Walnut Creek was adopted as an infant from India. Along with the rest of us, Kari's looking forward to seeing Mother Teresa today."

Then a man in a clerical collar approached us. "May I take your picture? I don't know who you are but you must be famous!"

Next, the Sisters of Missionaries of Charity from San Francisco filed in front of us. Two dark Indian faces beamed their smiles in our direction.

"Why don't you go and say hello to them? Show them your picture Kari." Full of enthusiasm, and uninhibited by their youth, our kids dashed to their side.

"We talked to their leader," Resa breathlessly reported. "She said that when Mother Teresa is done talking, they'll try to help us meet her."

Finally, the diminutive nun took the stage and bowed humbly to the people who packed the auditorium and to the dignitaries who shared the stage.

We hung on each word she spoke and joined in the prolonged standing ovation that displayed our collective love and admiration of her life of servanthood.

Ushered from the stage by a police guard, throngs of people desperately reached out to touch her as she quickly disappeared through the side door. Suddenly, before we knew it, the sisters from San Francisco whisked by and grabbed our children's hands. And they *all* followed Mother Teresa through the side door. When Neal and I approached, they *closed the door!*

"But those are our children in there," we appealed to the burly policeman stationed in front of the door.

"Well, I think they're safe with her."

"I know, but they might come out with that blue and white scarf on their head," I laughingly whined.

"She pinched our cheeks and asked us how we were," reported Kari. "She liked seeing the picture and said to work hard in school. And she asked David how he's doing with his braces."

"So we have no pictures, only loving memories. But the *presence of Jesus* was so real to me at the moment that I didn't mind being on the "other side" of the door. I marveled at how He had guided our steps. And I whole-heartedly agreed with Neal: *With Jesus, you don't need a banner!*

40

Ask any Mom or Dad...having children brings frustration! But the rewards are plentiful as well. To parent any child takes courage, commitment, patience, and most of all a sense of humor. My key ring shouts a reminder, "WHY LET REALITY WRECK YOUR DAY?" Every day has it's challenges.

"Therefore do not worry about tomorrow, for tomorrow will worry about itself. Each day has enough trouble of it's own" (Matthew 6:34).

We've experienced the normal growing pains and teenage annoyances. "Neal I think you'd better go downstairs and kiss your daughter goodnight."

"What daughter? Her bed's empty," Neal announced as he clomped back up the wooden stairs.

Such a pain! Her, "Oh-I'm-so-tired," punctuated by a giant stretch, was a clue. "I think I'll go to bed early tonight." But her spontaneous kiss really tied it up. Through our diligence and a phone call or two she came right home.

One of *our* best moments came when Neal, in bathrobe attire, and camouflaged by the inky night, hid behind the immense pine tree in our front yard. Soon a car slowed and she jumped out down the street. Daintily grasping her little shoes and running on tip toe, she neared the window. Neal held his breath as she reached to slide it open.

"Going somewhere sweetheart?" Neal hissed as he switched on his lantern.

Later behind our door, Neal and I stifled guffaws as we relived the scene. "Oh, you should have seen the look on her face – definitely unforgettable."

The next day I took a stern approach, "If you keep crawling out your window, we're going to have to nail it shut."

I had reached the end of my patience. Fortunately, the warning seemed to be enough for her.

So, with that and many other incidents, we "paid our dues" to the normal adolescent angst, and a few things worse than "normal".... nine times! And throughout it all, I've prided myself on being a "mean mother!" as this well known prose explains:

> "My mother insisted on knowing where we were at all times. You'd think we were on a chain gang or something. She had to know where we were and who our friends were.
>
> I'm ashamed to admit it, but she actually had the nerve to break the child labor law. She made us work. We had to wash dishes, make the beds and learn to cook. That woman must have stayed up nights thinking up things for us to do. And she insisted that we tell the truth, and nothing but the truth.
>
> By the time we were teenagers, she was much wiser and our life became unbearable. None of this tooting the car horn for us to come running; she embarrassed us to no end by insisting that friends come to the door to get us.
>
> I forgot to mention that most of our friends were allowed to date at the mature age of twelve or thirteen, but our old fashioned Mother refused to let us date until we were sixteen. She really raised a bunch of squares....
>
> I am trying to raise my children to stand a little straighter and taller and I am secretly tickled to pieces when my children call me mean. I thank God for giving me the meanest Mother in the World.... Our country needs more mean Mothers like mine. Blessing on that wonderful woman."

("Meanest Mother in the World" Author Unknown)

Being a parent and a "mean mom" is hard work! It's a full time job. But we found that parenting a child with special needs sometimes takes a little "extra" from the beginning. And in some cases it takes a lot extra. Acceptance and persistence are important qualities for parents to develop. "Treat your child like he's the best person in the world, and people usually follow suit," I advised.

Rosalie's new baby boy was born with Down Syndrome. "You'll need to speak up for him Rose. Kids with special challenges count on their parents for everything. Good school programs aren't a given. Then they need the right medical care and even recreational activities." Just the normal role as a parent, *plus!*

An example of this came when David was in Jr. High school. He was ecstatic that his concert band was traveling to San Francisco to see "Les Miserables." After school sessions acquainted the students with the story and the score. David was "stoked!"

But on Tuesday afternoon before the Sunday matinee date the teacher ran out to meet my car. "The theater has no elevators," he breathlessly announced. With crutches and leg braces and a strong upper body, David could do stairs, but four flights in a crowd wasn't workable. "And the seats in the wheelchair section are twenty-five dollars!"

"OK, I'll call them. But there isn't much time." I wasn't a happy camper! "Why do they expect David to pay nine dollars more than everyone else and then sit on the ground floor by himself?" The class had balcony seats. And with the city's recent 7.1 earthquake, it was unwise for David to sit alone.

So I called the theater. I guess I was wrong to *expect* a voice of reason on the other end. First, "Will you please hold?"...forever. Then, a pleasant, "The box office manager will call you back." That was OK, but it never happened. Many more calls, more promises and *no calls back!*

Out of frustration, I did the unthinkable. "David, maybe you shouldn't even go. It's such a hassle." "No way Mom. I *want* to go! I've been to all the meetings." Good for David. His spunk and determination spurred me on. But how many other people give up and go away?

Friday was my last chance. By now I was grasping at straws. I called San Francisco city offices, and searched for disability rights groups. Finally, in desperation, I called our Congressman's local office. "All I want is for David to sit somewhere without stairs. Wherever they want to put him is okay. And I want him to pay the student rate. After all, it's not his fault the theater doesn't have elevators. And for safety, he'll need someone to sit with him."

"You're entirely right. I can't believe the runaround you've been getting. I'll call the theater right away." The aide's response was gratifying. *She* called the theater. And in a flash *they* called me! "Mrs. Satre, this is the ticket manager. I'm so sorry that you've been having such a problem. We'll be glad to give your son two box seats at the student rate. In fact, the sixteen dollars he's already paid will cover both seats."

David loved "Les Miz!" Now his favorite line is, "Don't mess with my Mom or she'll call the Congressman!"

✤ 41 ✤

"Our children are all so different. How could we *not* recognize their individuality?" I implored.

"Well, even our twins are nothing alike."

We regularly remind each other, "Life doesn't come with guarantees...especially as parents."

Neal was always practical, "Even the kids born to us can have problems Jeannie. An accident could leave any of <u>them</u> disabled."

Thinking of Doug's rock climbing and other escapades, I heartily agreed. "That's the truth! We all have problems, but some of the things that handicap us just don't *show*."

"When we adopted, our kids already had their disability. We could only *help* them," Neal emoted. "So for us, it's love, and care. We'll give them the best chance they can have." I ended his sentence.

"We can't change the way their lives started. But we *can* help them change the way they finish!" What a gift to have a husband with such a positive attitude. Neal and I usually seemed able to balance each other.

Carol Turkington, a mother of a child with special needs expresses the adjustment we need to make in our expectations. Her article is called, "Welcome to Holland"

When you're going to have (or I say, adopt) a baby it's like planning a vacation to Italy. You're excited. You get a bunch of guidebooks, you learn a few phrases so you can get around, and then it comes time to pack your bags and head for the airport. Only when you land, the stewardess says "Welcome to Holland."

You look at one another in disbelief and shock, saying, "Holland? What are you talking about? I signed up for Italy."

"But", they explain, "there's been a change of plans. You've landed in Holland, and there you must stay!"

"But I don't know anything about Holland," you say. "I don't *want* to stay!"

But stay you do. You go out and buy some new guidebooks, you learn some new phrases and you meet people you never knew existed. The important thing is that you are not in a slum full of pestilence and famine. You're simply in a different place than you had planned. It's slower paced than Italy, less flashy than Italy, but after you've been there a little while and you have a chance to catch your breath, you begin to discover that Holland has windmills. Holland has tulips. Holland has Rembrandts.

But everyone else you know is busy coming and going from Italy. They're all bragging about what a great time they had there, and for the rest of your life, you'll say "Yes, that's what I had planned."

The pain of that will never go away. You have to accept that pain, because the loss of that dream, the loss of that plan, is a very, very significant loss. But if you spend your life mourning the fact that you didn't go to Italy, you will never be free to enjoy the very special, the very lovely things about Holland."[10]

In adoption you may know a lot about the physical situation of your child. You have a choice. We did. But we still had to face the facts. The accomplishments of our children, were often *different* than those of our friends' children. So we learned to celebrate diversity! Staying close to the Lord, being flexible and trying to be positive in parenting and *in life* has always been "it" for us.

When the children were young, I did my best to smooth the way for them. Sharing "our family" with the children's classes was fun for me. "Mom, Mrs. Steckbeck says you can come on Friday and bring your big pictures," Resa emoted. "Then Kari's class wants you next." This was an *occasion* for them and for me. Large color photos keenly illustrated the joy of our kids and family...Kari with Mother Teresa. Resa in the hospital in traction, smiling away! David in his spika cast which started at his waist and stretched to the tip of his toes. Stephen in India. These pictures couldn't help but soften hearts and teach kids in school acceptance for the physically challenged.

Just the presence of our family seemed to be a kind of travelling "consciousness raising group." Especially our summer vacations at the lake. David unstrapping his braces and then crawling to the water on hands and flat feet, rear in the air. And Rebecca being carried limply to the raft and all the others whooping it up on the beach. I vainly attempted to contain the gear of nine enthusiastic kids. Instead we littered the beach with mats, towels, buckets, shovels, air mattresses, shoes, socks, shorts, beach chairs and more. Added to this were two pairs of crutches, long leg braces, a wheelchair and sometimes a wagon. "Ah, the good 'ol days!" I can't say that I miss that part. But we're not the only ones. We have a lot in common with many other families like ours.

Besides acceptance of themselves and their differences, we've also encouraged a pride and identification with our children's birth countries. We've included their original name or other ethnic name as part of their new American ones. And we took field trips. "But I think the kids like the restaurants best," Neal concurred. Art exhibits, literature and friendships with people from their home countries have rounded out our efforts.

And we celebrated special days. "Do you want cookies or cupcakes?" Thirty two hungry kids were anxious to celebrate. Especially when the kids were young, the anniversary of their arrival into our family turned into an event.

Even now, Lia often calls *me* on Feb. 22, "So, do you know what day this is Mom?"

Celebrating anniversaries intrigued the other classmates and highlighted the special nature of adoption. But one little girl in first grade said to Lia, "I didn't know you were *married!*"

And then a couple of teachers really knocked themselves out. In second grade Lia's class prepared and ate a full Korean meal. "Mom, what are lentils?" David shouted across the grocery aisle. Cooking and serving them to his junior high class made his report on India come alive. And slide shows of India and Mother Teresa's children's home were *derigueur*.

We have done the best we could with the resources available to us. Other areas of the country currently have heritage camps for adopted children...a fun opportunity that we missed. But, as with many things in parenting, *in spite of us*, most of our children seem to have a strong sense of themselves and of their backgrounds. Their favorite stories have been of their arrivals. Over and over again we've joyfully relived them with enthusiasm!

Feelings of "abandonment" seem to be common in adoptees...especially during teen years. We don't believe in "pat answers," but how fortunate we are to be able to refer to God's word. "We're *all* adopted into God's family according to the kind intention of His will." So adoption has a very positive connotation for all members of our household.

Most of our children have generally cheerful and outgoing temperaments. But, as each of them works out their adult selves and finds their place in the world, adoption is likely to be part of the equation. We'll be there to encourage them.

42

Initially we reached out to children. Now our kids have led *us* into branching out. Derek spent every high school summer overseas. We remember when he came to Neal in sixth grade, "Dad, I'm signing up for a foreign language. I think I'll take French."

"Derek, we live in California. I'll take you to Mexico. You'll never go to France!" Neal was convinced.

Well, Derek took French. And after his freshman year in high school we took him to the airport. First "boot camp" in Florida then a *whole summer in France* working with Teen Missions. Norway, China and Japan followed.

Doug had his turn too. Leading Bible clubs in housing projects in South Central Los Angeles and evangelizing in North Africa *kept me on my knees.* "How could you *let* Doug do that?" my friend's would implore.

"What do you mean 'let'? He's an adult. He doesn't *ask* me!" Now I feel that way about his rock climbing and other outdoor adventures.

All of our kids have enjoyed mission trips to Mexicali, Mexico. Kari and David also helped build a church in Belgium. And Mindy spent a college summer in Poland with InterVarsity.

When Kari and Resa were eight, Vidya came to visit. "Mrs. Satre, this is Holt in Oregon. We know you're a long time Holt family and I hope you can help us out."

"Another child?" ran through my mind. So I was relieved to hear the rest.

"We have a social worker from India coming to San Francisco. She's escorting twin babies to their family there. But she needs a place to stay before continuing to Oregon."

Deja vu....twin babies from India. How could I say "no?" But then reality struck. Where would I put her?

"Ah sure, we'd love to have her." I said with a laugh.

So we picked her up at the airport. But no twin babies! Visa problems. That was an old story. But here came Vidya, clad in a beautiful sari, her jet black hair falling down her back in a neat braid. Our children were mesmerized by her appearance and gentle manner. After we got home, Kari and Resa charted her every move. "Mom, Vidya just took her hair down," Kari whispered as she darted in and then out of the kitchen.

A few minutes later it was Resa's turn, "Mom Vidya's in the bathroom."

"You'd think we had the *Queen* here, Neal! The girls find her so fascinating."

We had such a great time with her that we eked out every last bit of sightseeing we could. "Vidya, you'll love this. I think we have time," I emoted as the doorman cleared our path through the heavy brass rimmed entry doors.

First the escalators and then the glass elevator whisked us to the top of the Hyatt. She was properly impressed, "I didn't want you to miss the view of San Francisco Bay from up here." You could tell Neal was proud of the city! And Vidya was quietly in awe.

But this wonderful moment provided her with a close call. "Last call to Eugene," resonated in the air as we ran to the gate. A quick, tearful good-bye and she was gone.

The last time we heard from her was many years ago:

Dear Neal, Jeenie (sic) and children,
I just cannot believe that three years have passed since I met you! The memories of you all and of your warm loving home are as fresh in my mind as if I have just returned from USA. I am very lazy as far as letter writing is concerned. Even if I do not

write to you, you are always there in my sweet memories. I always tell people about you and your family. I keep imagining about the children's development. I wish all of you a very long, happy and prosperous life. I have a very small house to host you all at my place. I hope you would like to visit India... and also Vidya's small house. I do not have words to express my feelings for you all.

  With love,

  Vidya

Vidya lives in our sweet memories too...and in our photo album. We would love to visit her and her house someday!

About three years later, our whole family became "Friendship Partners" for an international graduate student at the University of California. The "little kids" had a great time greeting Hoon from Korea. At the airport, small American flags waving in their little hands, heralded his arrival. "We hope you'll feel that our home is your "home away from home." You're always welcome here. We hope you'll join us for Thanksgiving and Christmas. Everyone will be home and we have a great time together!"

After three years Hoon graduated with an MBA and returned to Korea. He and his wife Soo-Young still visit us when they come to the United States. And we hope to visit Korea some day too. Prashant, from Bombay, followed Hoon. Then we reached out to two Asian women, Fie Fie from Singapore, and Aikiko from Japan. But it was our summer with Elena that really became a *family project!*

Again we crowded around the bleak customs door at the San Francisco airport. This had become a familiar scene for us. But this wasn't adoption. Now it was visitors, arriving on their own. Only two escorts for a group of ten exhausted youngsters arriving from Russia. And what a hectic scene! Interpreters jabbered away in Russian. Little kids whined, cried, and complained about the long wait. Sharing the excitement with nine other families from our church was fun. We tested our few Russian words on each other and related plans for sightseeing and family outings.

Expectantly, all video cameras were poised at the closed door. "I can't wait!" resounded in the halls. Each family was anxious to meet "their child" from the Chernobyl Children's Project.

All *we* had was a name and an age...."Elena, ten years old." Then as the children filed out of customs, one little girl caught my eye. As soon as I spotted "her" I fervently hoped that she would be ours.

"Boy these kids don't know what's in store for them. They'll have a great summer," Neal enthused.

"This is just what they need!" I responded. "A chance to play outside."

"Can you imagine being *inside* all the time? Their poor parents must go crazy too." Neal reflected on the grim reality of life in Chernobyl. "They even stay inside at school. What a life!"

"Just wait'll they go swimming. Seven weeks of fun and sunshine!" A much needed physical and emotional respite from life seeped in radiation.

"Do you think they really can go home with their immune systems improved?" I thought Neal would know.

"Well, I hope so. But who really knows!" Neal sounded skeptical.

Finally the leader approached us with a clip board and gestured into the crowd. "Look. She's the one," I shrieked. Was it possible? They matched this darling child with us.

I had prayed for a *responsive* and *enthusiastic* child. Elena was that and much, much more! I had chosen her because of her name..."Elena." A special name, reminding me of our long ago Mexican baby, Susan Elena, had created a "connection."

As we drove across the San Francisco/Oakland Bay Bridge she boldly spoke up in halting English, "Is bay or is ocean?" Her accent was substantial.

"Hey, English!" I whooped. What an unexpected plus. Still, our Russian dictionaries and phrase books were at the ready.

"I speak little bit English. Not goood. Two years in school," she explained. We all cheered our approval.

After sleeping off massive jet lag, Elena began to unveil her delightful but sometimes demanding personality. "Resa come here right now. I need you help me NOW!," she shrieked. She quickly learned from me that this was *not* the way to get help. Any problems we had with her were "kid problems" not cultural ones. So we treated her just like a member of our family and we had a riotous, great time. Elena's personality and sense of humor meshed perfectly with ours. And although she could sometimes be annoying, I can't remember when we've had so many laughs!

Three days after her arrival we took off on vacation. Mom, Dad, Kari, Resa, David, Stephen, Elena and dogs Bear and Schnitzel all crammed into our Ford Club wagon. We were sure the majestic Sierra Nevada Mountains would impress her.

"Look Elena!" We had three hours to point out the sights as we traveled through serene valley and foothill country. Cows, horses, farms and fields surrounded our two lane ribbon of asphalt. But, like Mindy years before, *she* wanted to *teach us!* "In Russian, Karrova (cow)," she said, rolling her r's. Kari diligently recorded it all phonetically and we had fun learning Russian words.

On the second day of our vacation we snaked our way back down the mountain. The kids loved being pulled behind Ron's boat. Making conversation, I asked, "Elena, how were you chosen to come to America?" With her bright mind and enthusiastic spirit, I thought it would be school.

"Oh no," she cheerfully replied. "It's my *heart*. I was in hospital for two weeks...in May." What a shock!

"And *we're* planning to whip her around the back of a water ski boat?" Neal laughed.

"Great, and now we'll try to kill the kid!" I moaned. But thankfully she lived through it. No ill effects.

Our family physician checked her out, "There's a click in her heart. But I don't see an immediate problem. I don't think it's anything major." So we proceeded to treat her as a healthy child. And the boat trip was the high point of her seven weeks with us. Even though the airport departure was wrenching and extremely tearful, Neal and I agreed, "We don't want to even be in the same country with Elena when *her* hormones kick-in!!"

Another child-led involvement came in the area of sports. "Who would have dreamed that I'd be shooting baskets from a wheelchair?" Neal laughed. "But I tell ya, it's a lot of fun!" A former national championship basketball player at University of California at Berkeley, the sport has continued to play a big role in Neal's life.

Derek, our tallest son, at 6'6" decided early on that daily 6 a.m. practices five days a week weren't worth his three minute playing time on the Frosh team. He opted out! Douglas, at 6'4" stayed with basketball in high school and was team captain his senior year. We loved watching him play. "What'll we do next year?" wondered Neal. We'd spent all of our Tuesday and Friday nights at the gym!

But ironically, it is David, 5' tall with long leg braces and crutches who *loves basketball!* The Bay Cruisers, their team in Berkeley, has provided Neal, Stephen (reluctant) and David with great times on the court and wonderful opportunities to participate in tournaments across the United States.

When David was a Senior we swelled with pride as we heard this announcement:

"Today, September 28, the Bay Cruisers are officially 'retiring' the uniform of David Satre #51. In the future, no Bay Cruiser basketball player may wear this number. This is in recognition of David's unique and outstanding talents both as an athlete and as a person. He continues to be in the top 10 nationally in scoring, shooting percentage and assists."

David beamed too!

43

As I seek to stay close to God and live for Him, I'm relieved and encouraged. He isn't looking for "Super Humans." Just ordinary people like me and Neal.

We've learned not to be *afraid* to be afraid. That's important. God can *use* "afraid!"

"It's amazing, God always stands with us!" Neal and I reflect on this often.

He means it when He says, "I will never leave you or forsake you" (Joshua 1:5).

"Jeannie, He's the only one we can count on. He'll never let us down. Everyone else is human." Neal's words were wise.

"God's opened the doors. Aren't you glad we went through them? What we'd have missed!" I emoted.

"But *He* prepared the path. It'd never work otherwise."

"And it hasn't *all* been joyous, you know." I slumped on the couch remembering the pain we'd felt over a child's bad choices. The consequences were hard for *all* of us. "It's been so awful. I hate pain. But God was there," I conceded.

"And, Neal, remember what Bobbe told me? She's had daughter problems too you know. She said, 'I was telling God…but she'll have *scars*.' And He said, 'So do *I* Bobbe.' Doesn't that give you chills?"

"And thank goodness for the Psalms."

"Yea, God and Hagen-das bars!" Neal tried to lighten my mood.

"It's not over yet. Our life sure isn't tied up with any pretty bow," I observed.

"Get used to it, honey! With nine kids, ten now with Kathryn (Doug's wife), this is probably as good as it'll get." Neal's words always evened me out.

"Well, we've had a wedding. That was wonderful." I reported enthusiastically. Even though I silently cringed remembering the worms crawling through the imported chocolates at the rehearsal dinner. *My* only event!

"But there'll be grandkids and illness. So much to mourn and celebrate. Jeannie, with so many kids we have a *great* opportunity for joy and suffering. Just think!"

"So baby...what's our choice?" I was resigned. "We'd better choose joy and let God take care of our future. He's doing it whether we 'let' or not!"

"But isn't it better when we get out of His way?" Neal's observations encouraged me. "Just living takes courage. So keep taking the first step. That's all we have to do, you know?"

"Yeah, yeah...80% of success is just showing up. We've done that all along. I guess we can keep it up," I agreed.

"No regrets and keep going! Well, maybe a little regret once in a while. No one's perfect."

Life is an adventure....sometimes wonderful, sometimes agonizing. Our path has involved lots of detours and a houseful of kids!

Dorothy Atwood DeBolt captures my heart when she says,

> "Once we knew about these children, how could we turn our backs on them? Someone had to take them and love them. Someone had to give them a chance in life. We did, and we did it because we wanted to, not because we were forced to....Then a strange and lovely thing happens with each child. The moment he or she comes into this home, we can't imagine the family without them."[11]

There are many different paths. Seize the opportunities. Take the challenges. Get involved. Who knows where God will lead!

Endnotes

1. Community Bible Study, The Gospel of Mark/Lesson 4, 1991, 103 Rowell Court, Fall Church, VA, p. 7.

2. Jan de Hartog, *The Children*, H. Wolff, New York, NY, 1968, p. 22.

3. Hope Edelman, *Motherless Daughters*, Dell Publishing Group, Inc., New York, NY, 1994.

4. *Contra Costa Times*, August 1978.

5. Clifford Berman,"The Better Way," "Breast Surgery to *Prevent* Cancer: the Big Dispute," *Good Housekeeping*, March 1981.

6. David Perlman, Science Editor, *San Francisco Chronicle*, 1980.

7. Berman, *Good Housekeeping*.

8. Adopt a Special Kid (adoption agency - see appendix). Neal and I served on the AASK Board of Directors.

9. Oswald Chambers, *My Utmost for His Highest*, Dodd, Mead & Co., Inc., 1935, p. 54.

10. Carol Turkington, "Welcome to Holland," Reprinted from Attention Deficit Hyperactivity Disorder of Texas Newsletter, vol. 2, Issue 3, 9/89.

11. Joseph P. Blank, *19 Steps Up the Mountain*, J.B. Lippincott Co., New York, 1976, p. 7.

Clayton's Card

WE ARE RESPONSIBLE FOR CHILDREN
who put chocolate fingers everywhere,
who like to be tickled,
who stomp in puddles and ruin their new pants,
who sneak Popsicles before supper,
who erase holes in Math workbooks,
who can never find their shoes.

WE ARE RESPONSIBLE FOR THOSE
who stare at photographers from behind barbed wire,
who can't bound down the street in a new pair of sneakers,
who never counted potatoes,
who are born in places we wouldn't be caught dead,
who never got to the circus,
who lived in an x-rated world.

WE ARE RESPONSIBLE FOR THOSE
who never get dessert,
who have no safe blankets to drag behind them,
who watch their parents watch them die,
who can't find any bread to steal,
who don't have any room to clean up,
whose pictures aren't on anybody's dresser,
whose monsters are real.

WE ARE RESPONSIBLE FOR CHILDREN
who spend their allowance before Tuesday,
who throw tantrums in the grocery store and pick at their
food,
who like ghost stories,
who shove dirty clothes under the bed, and never rinse out
the tub,
who get visits from the tooth fairy,
who don't like to be kissed in front of the carpool,

who squirm in church and scream in the phone,
whose tears we sometimes laugh at and whose smiles can
make us cry.

WE ARE RESPONSIBLE FOR THOSE
whose nightmares come in the daytime,
who will eat anything,
who have never seen a dentist,
who aren't spoiled by anybody,
who go to bed hungry and cry themselves to sleep,
who live and move, but have no being.

WE ARE RESPONSIBLE FOR CHILDREN
Who want to be carried and for those who must,
for those we never give up on and for those who don't get a
second chance,
For those we smother...and for those who will grab the hand
kind enough to offer it.

Author Unknown

A Special Tribute

When a child has a special need, there's always something to celebrate. Small accomplishments mean so much. Even a smile can be a triumph! Our nephew Joseph's life was a prime example of finding meaning in adversity. Christine, a friend of his family, wrote this tribute to him.

He sits in his mothers arms, quiet and unresponsive. His hair is cut in a little boy cut, parted down the side and beautifully groomed. His shorts are bright blue, and the patterned yellow and red shirt brings out the color in his cheeks and makes his dark brown eyes more remarkable. His skin has a youthful pink and healthy glow.

He is completely at the mercy of his mother for movement, food to eat, air to breathe. He has to be suctioned often to keep his airway clear, fed through a tube to give him nourishment. He is helpless.

Then she rocks him back and forth, her strong arms holding him upright, and as she gives him movement, he smiles and gurgles a little giggle in the bottom of his throat.

Many people would say that this child is an unnecessary being in our society and would have us institutionalize or euthanize him. "What good could this child do for anyone? How could he be of help to us? Don't we have to keep our society more perfect, taking away the ugly, disfigured or unuseful?

As I pondered these questions I thought again of the picture of this child in his mother's arms - completely helpless and dependent. I realized this is a perfect picture of how we are in the eyes of God, helpless in our sin, needing a savior to save us, and care for our every need. We need his strong arms to lift us up when we are helpless, to guide us and keep us from falling, to clear pathways to breathe a life of holiness into us. Our joy comes when we allow God to do this for us and respond to his direction and guidance willingly.

Through the obedience of this mother to care tenderly for her child, a willingness to take the ugly of the world and make it beautiful, we see how God takes our ugliness and makes us beautiful. Without this example in a perfect society, we wouldn't see the need for God, we would only see our goodness and beauty. We needed Joseph, much more than he needed us...A tribute of God's Grace and Love.
By Christine Hicks
(Used with permission)

Joesph died in his sleep when he was six years and two months old. His life *was* very significant! In such a short time he touched the hearts of many people.

During a time of "parental angst" I found this posted on the counseling center bulletin board at our church. It continues to be helpful to me and many of my friends.

To "Let Go" Takes Love

To "let go" does not mean to stop caring, it means that I can't do it for someone else.

To "let go" is not to cut myself off, it is the realization that I can't control another.

To "let go" is not to enable, but to allow learning from natural consequences.

To "let go" is to admit powerlessness, which means that the outcome is not in my hands.

To "let go" is not to try to change or blame another, it is to make the most of myself.

To "let go" is not to care for, but to care about.

To "let go" is not to judge, but to allow another to be a human being.

To "let go" is not to be in the middle arranging all the outcomes but to allow others to effect their own destinies.

To "let go" is not to be protective, it is to permit another to face reality.

To "let go" is not to deny, but to accept.

To "let go" is not to nag, scold, or argue, but instead to search out my own shortcomings and to correct them.

To "let go" is not to adjust everything to my desires but to take each day as it comes, and to cherish myself in it.

To "let go" is not to criticize and regulate anybody but to try to become what I dream I can be.

To "let go" is not to regret the past, but to grow and to live for the future.

To "let go" is to fear less and to love more.

Author Unknown

Where Are They Now?

DOUGLAS - Married to Kathryn, M.Div. from Fuller Theological Seminary. Senior Pastor at the American Protestant Church in Bonn, Germany!

DEREK - Masters Degree from Cambridge University (Jesus College), working on a Ph.D in Psychology with an emphasis in Geriatrics (perfect timing...for us!).

REBECCA - BA in Psychology, MA in Marriage, Family, Child Counseling. Leader in her church's "20 Something" group in Sacramento.

MINDY - BA in Recreational Therapy, works in a rehabilitation hospital with patients who have brain injuries. Leader in her church's "20 Something" group in Sacramento.

LIA - Married to Michael. BA in Political Science, teaching credential. Lives in San Diego at the beach!

KARl - Completed training in Computer Graphic Arts and works in business. Attends Campus Crusade.

RESA - Attends Community College in Sacramento. Working toward a teaching credential possibly in Special Education. Studying sign language and works with youth in church.

DAVID - Attends Community College and plays on a semi-professional wheelchair basketball team. Is serving as Jr. High Intern at a Community Church.

STEPHEN - Attends Community College. Drummer and guitar player/singer in a Christian band. Drummer for Saturday night church service. Writes Christian music.

Scriptures That Encouraged
Our Adoptions

Proverbs 3:27 Do not withhold good from those who deserve it, when it is in your power to act.

Proverbs 16:9 We can make our plans, but the Lord determines our steps. (NLT)

Proverbs 21:13 If a man shuts his ears to the cry of the poor, he too will cry out and not be answered.

Proverbs 25:25 Like cold water to a weary soul is good news from a distant land.

Isaiah 40:29 He gives strength to the weary, and to him who lacks might, He increases power. (NASB)

Isaiah 40:31 Yet those who wait for the Lord will gain new strength; they will mount up with wings like eagles, they will run and not get tired, they will walk and not become weary. (NASB)

Galatians 6:9 Let us not become weary in doing good, for at the proper time we will reap a harvest if we do not give up.

Galatians 6:10 Therefore, as we have opportunity, let us do good to all people, especially to those who belong to the family of believers.

2 Thessalonians 1:11 That our God may count you worthy of your calling, and fulfill every desire for goodness and the work of faith with power. (NASB)

2 Thessalonians 3:13 Do not grow weary of doing good. (NASB)

Appendix

The Adoption Process

1. Make your initial inquiry at adoption agencies dealing with the type of child and countries of origin that interest you.
2. Attend the agency's group meeting of prospective adoptive parents. Don't let anything they might say *discourage you!*
3. The group meeting will provide you with an opportunity to see representative pictures of children the agency serves. You will meet social workers, other parents, and hear a rundown of the adoption procedure.
4. If you are single, choose an agency that is willing/eager to work with you.
5. Apply to the agency of your choice for the sex, age and nationality of the child that you feel will fit in with your family. This doesn't have to be firm. Your ideas can/will be explored with your social worker.
6. Each foreign country has it's own requirements. Some will only allow childless couples to adopt. Some have strict age requirements, others deal only with couples and some require travel and a length of stay in the country (weeks/months). Most agencies deal with several countries.
7. Decide on at least three references who know you well and are supportive of your adoption quest.
8. At the *same time* apply for your homestudy with the agency that is *licensed in your state* for inter-country adoption. This agency may be the same or, as in our cases, different. There can be a considerable wait to start the homestudy, depending on case loads. So it is good to "get in line."
9. Make an appointment for the required physical exam for each of you.

10. DON'T STRESS! Social workers are people too. The horror stories of "white glove" inspections hopefully are a thing of the past. For the most part, they want you to be successful too. (But coffee and cookies won't hurt.)

11. Be prepared. Explore your feelings with your spouse (or family, if you're single) *before* the social worker's first visit. (You have probably already done this anyway.) "Why do you want this child?" or, as in our case, "Why do you feel the *need* for another child?" Consider the racial aspect.

12. Although possibly valid to you, asking for a play-mate for your current child is often frowned upon. Most agencies stress finding the best home for the *child*. They want to make sure you want the child for *himself/herself.*

13. If you are a prospective single parent, your extended family and areas of moral support will be important.

14. Be confident! Think of all you have to offer a child. Love and the security of one's *own family* is much more important than a wealth of material possessions.

15. The homestudy usually consists of a minimum of four visits. This will all depend on *your* state's requirements. At least one or two visits will be in your home with both of you (and your children) present.

16. At least one visit will be with each of you individually. Be prepared to discuss infertility if that is an issue.

17. The social worker will guide you through the maze of necessary official forms. The 1-600 and your fingerprints, both needed for the Department of Immigration, are the primary ones.

18. Realize that agencies and social workers are often overloaded and understaffed. Try not to get frustrated. But if you feel forgotten call them to remind them of your existence.

19. Develop patience as you wait for that all important picture of *your child!*

20. The picture and information about the child will arrive at the agency. When you both meet at their office you will get to "meet" your child for the first time. You will then decide on the basis of the photo and the sometimes lim-

ited information if this is a good match for you and your family.

21. If, for some reason, you don't feel comfortable with the particular choice, the wait will begin again and another child may be chosen.

22. Once you decide, the agency starts getting the visa and travel plans and, if needed, escorts in order. Remember, there are at least three offices involved: your local agency, the agency overseas, and the Department of Immigration.

23. Another *wait* can ensue between getting the picture and your child's arrival. If the child is three or older, this is a good time to send them pictures of your family, your home, his room, and family pets. This will help acquaint him/her with what is certain to be a new adventure and adjustment.

24. Familiarize yourself with a few basic phrases in his language. This can be invaluable to both of you. Simple language tapes are particularly helpful.

25. The call will *finally* come! Sometimes you will have notice of flight arrival a week, or even less, in advance. Now get going! Take time off work for these very special days.

At the Airport

1. The airport scene is an *exciting* one! You will join your social worker, other parents and, sometimes, agency volunteers.
2. After the plane lands the volunteers will escort the children through disembarcation and Customs. Through the glass wall that divides you, you will see your child for the first time!
3. If this is the first landing in the U.S. the children will proceed directly to Customs (if not, you are *lucky* and will be able to claim your child immediately.)
4. You will wait outside of Customs until your name is called (be sure to bring things to entertain any siblings). This delay can be an hour or more depending on the foreign air traffic.
5. In my experience only one parent was allowed into the strictly controlled Customs area. You will finally get to meet your child face to face. You may get to thank the escort who cared for him for many exhausting travel hours as well as the volunteer. You sign documents and leave with your new family member.
6. It may be difficult, but try to keep your greeting with other family members low key. A lot of commotion, flash bulbs and shrieks can bewilder or even frighten an already tired and confused child or baby.
7. The ride home can be peaceful or harrowing depending on the distance and the temperament of your child. Ours, so exhausted from the flight, usually fell immediately asleep.

Post Arrival

1. After arriving home, be relaxed and patient. It may take a while for your child to adjust to a new sleep/wake schedule.
2. Keep foods simple: chicken noodle soup or rice, crackers etc. If you have an older child from Korea, kimchee is a big hit. They sometimes have a voracious appetite. Take your cues from them.
3. Treat for head lice if your child has lived in a children's home.
4. Make an appointment with your family doctor or pediatrician for a physical exam. Start or continue series of childhood inoculations. Have child tested for parasites. Ask about hepatitis B.
5. Look forward to a few more visits from your social worker. "Sing the praises" of your new child and/or ask questions.
6. Later (months) file papers for finalizing your adoption. You may or may not need an attorney to do this. Your social worker will inform you of your options. This will be followed by a special visit to the Judge!
7. You may now file for citizenship (Naturalization) at the time the adoption is finalized.
8. Join (or start!) an adoption support group to get to know other families with children adopted internationally. It is especially helpful for older siblings to get to know families like theirs.
9. Consider subscribing to a magazine specializing in intercountry adoption. The articles alone are extremely helpful and informative. (See Appendix.)

Considering a Child
With Special Needs

1. There are several different areas that designate a child as "special needs." They include age, being part of a sibling group, race, mixed race, abuse and disability.
2. Disabilities vary from very minor and/or correctable to more severe and permanent. So after exploring your ideas with your social worker, you can decide on the level of involvement you feel able to tackle. Don't sell yourself short!
3. Deciding on a child with special needs can be very rewarding! Most children seem to blossom in their new homes, but "challenged" kids often progress *far beyond* what is expected of them.
4. When you say "yes" to a child with special needs you open your home and heart to a child who may not be chosen or who will have a much longer wait....especially longer than a healthy infant.
5. Agencies will sometimes adjust their fees to help facilitate adoption of kids with special needs.
6. Don't let predicted medical expenses automatically rule you out. State children's assistance programs will often cover the medical expenses of a child with a pre-existing medical problem. Check with *your state.*
7. Check to see what your medical insurance will cover. Companies often start coverage after the adoption is finalized.
8. Explore educational and support services in your community. Respite care is sometimes available if your child has at least a moderate challenge.
9. Contact a professional or another parent who has experience with the type of child or special need you're considering. Fear and doubts are often easily dispelled by a knowledgeable and enthusiastic parent.

10. Realize that the medical community may tend to be negative. Take their counsel but don't be discouraged. Kids fool doctors on a regular basis!
11. *Be encouraged!* Parenting a child with special needs can be a great experience if you have a positive attitude and are willing to be "stretched."
12. You will meet people you wouldn't otherwise know and you will be exposed to enriching areas of life as you meet the needs of your child.
13. With your guidance, siblings can develop a compassion and understanding they might not have learned any other way. With the right attitude, the whole family will benefit!

Helpful Resources

1. **Adoptive Families of America**
   3333 Highway 100 North
   Minneapolis, MN 55422
   (800) 372-3300

   Can refer you to your local adoptive-parent support group.
   Lists agencies by states. Will send you how-to information
   and its magazine: *Adoptive Families* is very helpful!

2. **"AASK" - Adopt a Special Kid**
   287 17th Street   Suite 207
   Oakland, CA 94612
   (510) 451-1748

3. **"AASK America" - Adopt a Special Kid**
   226 4th Street NE
   Washington, D.C. 20002
   (202) 544-3603

4. **Bay Area Adoption Services**
   465 Fairchild Drive,   Suite 215
   Mountain View, CA 94043
   (650) 964-3800   Fax: (650) 964-6467
   (International Adoption)

5. **Holt International Children's Services**
   P.O. Box 2880
   Eugene, OR 97402
   (541) 687-2202
   E-Mail: info@holtintl.org
   Website: http://www.holtintl.org

   (Ask for their magazine *Hi Families!*)

6. **The National Adoption Information Clearinghouse**
    5640 Nicholson Lane, Suite 300
    Rockville, MD 20852
    (301) 231-6512

    Makes referrals and sends free fact sheets.

7. *The Adoption Resource Book,* **by Lois Gilman,**
    published by HarperCollins, 1992.

8. **Internet: Frequently Asked Questions for Adoptive
    Parents:** http://nysernet.org/cyber/adoption/others.html

To Sponsor a Child

1. **World Vision**
    Box 70104
    Tacoma, WA 98481-0104
    (800) 777-5777

    International relief/support services to children and families. Monthly sponsorship or one time gift.

2. **Holt International Children's Services**
    Box 2880
    Eugene, OR 97402
    (541) 687-2202
    E-Mail: info@holtintl.org

3. **Christian Children's Fund**
    1-800-501-9779

Order Form

Postal orders:
Jeannie Satre, 401 Gregory Lane, Suite 112 Pleasant Hill, CA 94523

Telephone orders: (800) 931-BOOK (2665)

Please send *Eight Was Not Enough to*:

Name:_____

Address:_____

City:_____ State:_____

Zip:_____

Telephone: (_____) _____

Book Price: $11.00 in U.S. dollars.

Sales Tax: Please add 8.25% for books shipped to a California address.

Shipping: $4.00 for the first book and $1.00 for each additional book to cover shipping and handling within US, Canada, and Mexico. International orders add $7.00 for the first book and $3.00 for each additional book.

Quantity Discounts Available - Please call for information
(925) 939-1991